No Matter

How Dark

the Valley

No Matter How Dark the Valley

THE POWER OF FAITH IN TIMES OF NEED

G. Don Gilmore

1817

Harper & Row, Publishers, San Francisco
Cambridge, Hagerstown, New York, Philadelphia
London, Mexico City, São Paulo, Sydney

All Scripture quotations, unless otherwise noted, are from the Revised Standard Version of the Bible, copyrighted 1946, 1952, © 1971, 1973.

NO MATTER HOW DARK THE VALLEY: *The Power of Faith in Times of Need.* Copyright © 1982 by G. Don Gilmore. All rights reserved. Printed in the United States of America. No part of this book may be used or reproduced in any manner whatsoever without written permission except in the case of brief quotations embodied in critical articles and reviews. For information address Harper & Row, Publishers, Inc., 10 East 53rd Street, New York, NY 10022. Published simultaneously in Canada by Fitzhenry & Whiteside, Limited, Toronto.

FIRST EDITION

Designer: Jim Mennick

Library of Congress Cataloging in Publication Data

Gilmore, G. Don.
   NO MATTER HOW DARK THE VALLEY

  1. Suffering. 2. Faith. I. Title
BV4905.2.G53 1982   248.8'6   81-48208
ISBN 0-06-063121-X   AACR2

---

82 83 84 85 86 10 9 8 7 6 5 4 3 2 1

For
Joseph R. Edington,
"Friend in Deed"

Contents

Introduction: Through the Valley   ix

1. The Pathway of Faith   1
2. The Pathway of the Soul   18
3. The Pathway of the Kingdom   36
4. The Pathway of Love's Lessons   56
5. The Pathway of Prayer   75
6. The Pathway of Hope   103

Index   129

Introduction: Through the Valley

WHEN PERSONAL crisis strikes, the first thing we want to know is where we can get emergency relief. We want help—the swifter and more uncomplicated the better. Many of us begin dipping into the Bible in search of a verse of scripture that will speak specifically to our problem. Some engage in midnight prayer vigils, day-long pleading, and bargaining with God. Some embark on frantic shopping sprees, searching for just the right church, minister, healer, prophet, theology, or group to meet the immediate need.

However helpful any of these short-term solutions may appear, I have come to the conclusion that the secret of overcoming a crisis is the direct result of personal companionship with our Lord, who not only lived triumphantly through his own crisis times but in spirit reveals pathways through our darkest moments as well. Surely it is not so improbable that, if God is spirit and we have capacity to share that spirit, there should be an intimate sharing between us. I sometimes remind people that, when praying for help, we must not think it strange if something actually does come to us that we would not ordinarily have considered. The fact is that scattered through the gospel record are a number of specific references to Jesus' way of responding to crisis. I am convinced that the spirit of Jesus is available to us at this very moment—at *any* moment—to help us through the "test" periods of our lives. "Even though I walk through the valley of the shadow of death..." (Ps. 23:4)—the Psalmist, wise in the ways of God, knew beyond any question that he would be led through the dark valley into the light on the other side. The spirit of Jesus living in and through us is our good shepherd, and he leads us on specific paths through troubled times.

Think of the times you've been in the trenches of a crisis battle, anxiously speculating on how much longer the wretched trial would last. There are those who confidently declare that we are born to such trouble, that this is the human condition. They insist that the only way God can teach us is through suffering. I have no quarrel with the idea that suffering is a formidable instructor, but it is not the consummate teacher. The essence of Christ's teachings, including his strategies for crisis, is not how to get by in life with a minimum of pain but rather how to overcome, to transcend personal suffering. Jesus gives us a challenge that is thrillingly personal: "I came that [you] might have life, and have it abundantly" (John 10:10).

In the material you are about to read, I will of course be putting you in touch with the things Jesus said in isolated sermons, conversations, and comments. But if I've done my job adequately, you will find yourself increasingly in touch with the "mind of Christ" (Phil. 2:5), which is our contemporary and through which flows information that can be acted on in times of trouble.

I recently counseled a Christian man who wanted me to share his pain in a harsh crisis event. Gradually I became aware of the spiritual help that was gathering, that was in fact being galvanized to his need. I tried to direct his attention to a specific redemptive guidance that seemed inspired by Christ's triumphant presence, but my friend wasn't ready for that. He wanted me to join him in hanging on a cross because, as he put it, that's what Jesus had to do. Understanding his state of mind, and not wanting to appear critical or unsympathetic, I did have to point out that Jesus deliberately chose the way of the cross. The suffering he endured was totally voluntary. Crisis times, because they are foisted on us, are usually not cross events; more often they are lessons in transcendence disguised as dilemmas awaiting the application of Christ's one-to-one guidance.

I want to emphasize that the leadings of Christ for living through crisis are drawn to us by our need. Remember, God loves us and on a practical level all the difficult "tests" of life can be worked through as we receive his love to the degree that we are capable in consciousness of receiving it. The guidance patterns offered in the New Testament are not blueprints for our behavior; each crisis situation is unique. Yet when we grow into a sharing of the Christ spirit that made Jesus what he was, we are in touch with power that can overcome, no matter how dark our valley experience.

Don't misunderstand me: what I'm asking you to consider is not a spiritual panacea or a holy anesthetic guaranteed to give a few hours of relief. Sometimes crisis storms will continue to rage even after we've come under guidance. Then we have but one course of action, and it is all the more crucial. We must continue to be obedient to Christ's direction and companionship, for he alone can eventually deliver us. A veteran of innumerable crises, St. Paul once expressed the ultimate value of persevering in Spirit: "We know that all things work together for good" (Rom. 8:28) because, as he put it with personal feeling, "I know whom I have believed" (2 Tim. 1:12). That's the heart of the matter! When we know him—really know him—whatever the crisis may be, we are always in touch with the master who came so that we might have an abundant life.

CHAPTER 1

The Pathway of Faith

LATE ONE Thursday afternoon, I was wheeled into the emergency room of the Holy Family Hospital blood-spattered, bruised, and in shock. I had been out running earlier, and along the way had encountered my old nemesis, a belligerent Great Dane watchdog who had menaced me nearly every day for the past two years. Always before, despite a disturbing show of violence, he would grudgingly let me pass. But on that particular afternoon, for some reason or unreason, he decided to attack me.

The sight of that huge animal suddenly charging across the road, eyes coldly fixed, teeth bared for action, lunging his 160-pound body projectile-like at my throat, is a nightmare moment I'm still trying to forget. My only defense was to thrust my arm in his direction, attempting as best I could to protect my face—which was like throwing a piece of meat to a shark. He grabbed my arm just below the elbow and began shaking it so ferociously I screamed in pain and terror. After what seemed an eternity of mauling and twisting, he backed off. I'm still not sure what diverted his attention, whether it was my ear-piercing cries or the sudden arrival of his owners. Perhaps it was both. At any rate, the first crisis had passed and I was still alive.

I was eventually cleaned, stitched, given a shot of penicillin, and sent home. Two days later, an orthopedic surgeon would put my arm in a cast and there it would remain for two weeks. But arriving home from the hospital that first night, I stretched out on the sofa in our living room and began reflecting on the chain of events covering the past few hours. I was, as they say, trying to put the pieces back together. It was difficult not to relive the attack again and again. Strangely, I had no anger toward the dog or its owner; I was more dismayed at having been violated. I tried not to be anxious about my wounds, but that was nearly impossible when, only a short time before, I had been looking down at the exposed bone of my right arm laid bare beneath mangled tissue, wondering if I'd even have the use of it again. This was phase two of the crisis; the first being survival, the second concern about permanent injury.

After my family had gone to bed, I sat alone in the dark and searched for something, anything, to occupy my thoughts. Surveying the room, I noted several objects revealed in the moonlight flooding through our kitchen window. On a nearby table, I saw a book I had just finished reading. It was written by Dr. George Sheehan, a cardiologist, philosopher, and runner. The volume is filled with memorable passages. One that came to mind was a quotation from the philosopher William James, who declared that all of us live far below our energy potential. "What we now need," James insisted, is "the 'moral equivalent of war.'" In *The Varieties of Religious Ex-*

perience, Dr. James maintained that we need something "heroic" that will speak to us as universally as does war, yet will prove to be more compatible to our spiritual selves.[1] Like war, this would provide a setting, an arena to demonstrate the best that we can be, to use Dr. Sheehan's expression, "a theater of heroism."

For Sheehan and others like me, the marathon run is that theater; but I was to discover another one. Those long days and nights of stressful incapacity had become my crisis crucible of hurt and anxiety. For years I had proclaimed faith, but never before was I involved in a crisis that required such a demonstration of personal faith. Mark Twain once observed, "It's easy to be a Christian when you hold four aces in your hand." Did I have faith that, despite what appeared to be, I would somehow be cared for? Indeed, that I had a right to make such a claim in the first place? Even more, did I have sufficient faith to allow the spirit of God to do his healing work on my battered arm? Later, with my arm held high in a cast, I would attempt to cultivate faith the same way that I would customarily have been cultivating fear. Farmer-like, when we worry, we are sowing that which we shall eventually reap. The same thing can be said for faith. I deliberately attempted to cultivate my faith by visualizing, if I may mix my metaphors, successfully opening interior windows that were stuck tight with fear. I can't remember when it happened, but one day I became aware that I could consciously shut God out of this crisis, thus proving the power of my anxious outer self. Gradually, as I prayed, I began to realize that faith, as a gift of God, applied to my present crisis, was really the unreserved willingness to let God heal my arm despite whatever external negatives appeared in the picture. I cannot think of any other way of putting it except to say that I surrendered my arm to God in the sense of the New Testament character with the withered hand who extended his hand to Jesus to be healed (Luke 6:6–11). I was not conscious of any technique. It just seemed that I was being led to do this. The result was that I was released from anxiety. In fact, I cannot remember when I have been so relaxed while living through a crisis.

Several days later, when the cast was removed, my faith was dealt a dramatic blow at the sight of the wounded arm. At best, it looked alien. I kept thinking, Can this black and blue, stitched and shriveled thing belong to me? My optimistic doctor friend insisted that it did. "Don't worry," he said, "your arm is going to be just fine." To prove the point, he had me do some finger exercises, which I could barely manage. "See, look at that!" he bubbled. "You're going to get that arm back to normal. But there's one condition," he added, frowning a bit. "Whatever you do, don't baby it!" Babying meant taking it easy, avoiding risk, comforting and soothing the arm. Not babying meant doing exercises that pushed me through the pain barrier, stretching to the limit, seeing how much I could endure. It was as though I had surrendered my arm to God in faith, now he was giving it back to me in faith.

At this point, I was plunged into a third crisis. I felt a deep revulsion at the thought of pursuing pain for the sake of healing, though I knew it was necessary. I was also aware that the only obstacle to my total healing would be a weakness of my own resolve. There is a strange fascination that comes in beholding your own weakness. While you may know better, still the enervating sense of feebleness pleads wistfully, "I'm only human." A case in point is the New Testament story of Jesus' disciples failure to heal an epileptic boy (Matt. 17:14–

21). Now, I can easily identify with the feelings of those men as they marveled at their inability to do what at first they felt they could do. How difficult it must have been for them to accept their failure, having observed Jesus' successes in so many healing situations. Initially, they may have figured that it was just their humanity getting in the way. But Jesus explained that their failure was not due to being human; rather, it was due to their lack of faith—meaning that a demonstration of healing was well within their faith capacity but only faith, that total and complete opening to God to work in his own unique way, was missing.

When attacked by the Great Dane, my first thought was, How can this be happening to me? Having never been through such an experience, I marveled at my vulnerability. In those first days of physical therapy, I tried all sorts of ways to maintain a sense of God's presence. I kept up a reading vigil in the New Testament, carefully noting our Lord's estimate of people's capacity to overcome by faith. There is no gilding of the lily in the gospel record. Men and women are what they are in and out of crisis—often mediocre and undistinguished, sometimes tragically wed to the lowest common denominator. But when even the most ordinary and human of us, according to the Scripture, become aware through the power of faith that Christ is working in us right now, then the possibility and promise comes alive that we can become new people, healed of our infirmities, renewed and restored to a vital and effective life. But it can't be done alone. People must make the faith response that somehow, some way, they do belong to the higher order that is God.

As I began pumping new blood into my withered arm through the rigors of physical exercise, at the same time making increasing claims by faith, I was affirming that in God I do live and move and have my being. I gave a tour de force performance as I acted on what I believe concerning Christ's promise that by faith I could be made whole. I was saying, "Lord, I cannot do this alone, but with your strength I can push, pull, stretch, and pump my way all the way back to health. I affirm and believe that, despite the pain and all the appearance factors, you are working to restore my arm to complete use. I now open all my being to you—body, mind, and spirit. Thank you Father."

I'm happy to report that after only a few weeks of therapy my arm became as strong as ever. I must give credit where it is due. The physical therapy per se was a tremendously important part of my recovery; but I must say unreservedly that the way of faith that opened me to God's power to heal made the crucial difference. The Spirit did through me what I could not have done for myself, and in the process I was reminded not only of who I am, but more importantly *whose* I am. I learned that I am a dependent creature sustained by the power of God's spirit. Faith for me is no longer some vague, shallow trust in God. It is the application of God's guidance by faith to any of life's crises.

As I study the life of Jesus and some of those who in the intervening years have shared his spirit—particularly in times of crisis—I note a common characteristic. They are, for the most part, thoroughgoing empiricists. They hold the conviction that, by faith, God works through their personal experience, whatever the external conditions. They seek to remain (insofar as is possible) open and sensitive to God's presence, not as a romantic ideal but as a faithful response to the creator's direction, so that they can be more like what they were intended to be. In fact, they all but relish times of testing, for these represent battles to be fought and victories to be won. By Christlike faith they position themselves to channel God's presence from the inner and deeper spiritual realm to the outer physical order. This, they unquestioningly believe, will have an absolutely transforming effect on the problem-plagued outer scene.

The world, for them, is a theater; sometimes harmonious and beautiful, but often tragic, with crisis challenges of varying intensity. Responding to good theater is easy, but bad theater requires conscious effort. One maxim in response to bad theater is that under no circumstances must it ever be accepted as something God-given, nor should it be ignored as though it will go away. Unfortunately, through negative experience we often become so conditioned to bad scripts that we keep coming up with plausible rationalizations, thus making the negative tolerable if not respectable. The "faith empiricists," on the other hand, shop for new scripts as a way of life, which I will hereafter refer to as "making a faith response."

Faith refers to a growing process in which even the negative scripts seem more like challenges than obstacles. Whenever Jesus taught faith, he spoke of it in a very technical sense. For him, faith proceeds on the audacious assumption that you must live beyond yourself; and the more you feel at home with that which is beyond, the greater the creative energy is released through you. Faith is a particular attitude that puts you in touch with the higher creative energy of God which, while it is beyond you, works through you as from the higher to the lower levels.

Nothing irrelevant happens on the stage of this theater, though most players are tempted to think so. One afternoon our son David, wet from swimming, came running to meet my wife and me after we had been sailing. His face was pale, his words tumbling in torment. "My cross, my cross and chain—it got off from around my neck and I lost it!" "Where, David?" we asked. "Over there!" He pointed to a large swimming area roped off from the rest of the lake. People were everywhere. The water was murky from all their stirrings. I tried to resist the overwhelming feeling of futility. It was a crisis moment for David. How could something so small be recovered from such an impossible hiding place?

My wife, Natalie, answered simply, "The cross is yours and we'll find it!" She grew very quiet, then she marched almost military-like into the water. She looked alert, but not anxious. I knew she was praying—that is, she was making her inner faith connections, opening to the flow of recovery energy—visualizing, visualizing. In less than a minute, in which she moved no more than three or four feet in any direction, she looked at me and announced, "Here it is, under my foot!" Overjoyed, David plunged into the water and retrieved his cross and chain.

Fifteen, perhaps even ten years ago, I would have considered such a tale absolutely disgusting, demeaning to faith, reeking of exhibitionism. I would have rejected the spectacle of using the sacred vehicle of spiritual seeking for such a trivial end. I would have charged that praying for the recovery of a cross and chain, when compared with all the really critical needs across the world, is nothing less than a repulsive self-serving attempt to manipulate the power of God. So much for the hang-ups of a decade or so ago.

Today I would not only defend but openly advocate the legitimacy of taking on faith challenges of any magnitude. If by chance you are negative on this approach, then let me ask you a question. Please tell me where the minor leagues of faith and prayer are? Where do we really learn how to practice God's presence from the ground up? Where do we obtain the confidence-building faith experience that will equip us for the big leagues of great humanitarian effort? The truth is that for most people no such training ground exists—at least no allowance is made for it. The tragedy is that well-intentioned people believing in faith and prayer, when thrust into life-and-death crises, do pray, but unfortunately they do so faithlessly—that is, with reservations a mile long that God can't really be expected to help in this situation. Consequently, the results are negligible. There is no testimony to pious tradition more compelling than that Christian people, despite limited results in faithless prayer, continue to pray.

The problem as I see it is in the grass-roots faith and confidence-building efforts, or lack of them. People of the spirit of Jesus should regard their trials and tribulations, however small, as challenges whereby they are given the opportunity to prove their faith. The spiritual life is constructed on faith ventures. It travels from self to God, but it travels by faith in a reality larger than self to which the self can wholeheartedly make its surrender, having actually experienced the larger reality at work in everyday life—even in the midst of crisis. This is why spiritually alive people take on the "cross and chain" challenges that may seem to others sort of strange, or at least of little consequence. To these people, however, they are initiations in the order of faith development.

People frequently wonder why God seems so outrageously absent in catastrophic events—particularly where the most loyal are involved in suffering. The answer may be specifically involved with the faith responses we have or have not made in a variety of challenge situations. Day-by-day, we are establishing faith connections through which we can draw direct personal help in times of trouble. One of the significant benefits of faith-venturing is the unlearning of limitation concepts imposed by the external world, where the panic level is always high.

Those who make the little leaps of faith behold God at work in helping them find not only their crosses and chains, but other lost things of life like coins and wallets and keys and animals and needed parking places. More important, God is willing to help us recover our lost health and misplaced identities, our lost hopes, loves, dreams, aspirations, relationships, even our lost faith. The net result is an obedient faith that is proven through numerous testings. Faith is always open-eyed, adventurous, forward looking. To be sure, there will be times when some faith responses will be off target. But again, this is the way we learn and it comes only through experience.

I remember a millionaire salesman who shared with me what he called his "secret of success." He explained that on long sales trips he would purposely get off the expressways and travel through small towns, stopping frequently to call on sales-resistant merchants in independent variety stores and try to persuade them to buy a box of no. 2 lead pencils (which were, of course, the least of the things he had to sell). I asked him why he did this. He explained that this was his way of keeping a sharp edge on his sales skills. It was also a motivating factor in helping him feel the power at work.

Jesus once spoke glowingly of a man who revealed so great a faith that he "marveled" at him and declared he hadn't seen such a faith in all of Israel, which I assume included his own disciples. The man of such marvelous faith was a soldier, a Roman centurion who on this occasion had a servant that was ill. He approached Jesus through intermediaries, saying,

> Lord, do not trouble yourself, for I am not worthy to have you come under my roof; therefore I did not presume to come to you. But say the word, and let my servant be healed. For I am a man set under authority, with soldiers under me: and I say to one, "Go," and he goes; and to another, "Come," and he comes; and to my slave, Do this, and he does it. (Luke 7:6-8)

The centurion had spent his entire career working within a chain of command. He had implicit faith in the effectiveness of this command relationship because he had seen it successfully demonstrated in battles large and small. Therefore, in his moment of crisis, the centurion reverted to his conditioning as a soldier. He placed himself in the position of being low man on the faith-healing totem. He knew that, from this surbordinate position in the faith chain of command, he would be able to draw on the power and authority set over him. He did not have to initiate any orders. All he had to do was to carry them out. This centurion kind of faith rests on the confidence that God, as the supreme commander, will in good order transform the worst into the best. Faith, here, is a dynamic functioning attitude in that whatever the circumstances, one can have confidence in the power of a proven chain of command under the authority of God.

Those who make a faith response in crisis times are connecting with the inner spiritual dimensions that underlie the external world. It is like the theater within the theater; the perfect hidden within the imperfect; or, as Wordsworth put it, "That world within the world we see." This inner realm is what Jesus referred to as the Kingdom of God, which I shall discuss more fully in a later chapter. He made it very clear that the "inner" was distinct from the outer: "My Kingdom is not of this world." But he stated just as emphatically that each of us is in close proximity to the Kingdom because, as he declared, it is within us. The important thing to remember is that we are in working correspondence with the Kingdom of God, and, by that magnetic power of willingness we call faith, we can draw the inner spiritual energy to the outer crisis demand.

People who share the spirit of Jesus and exercise their faith options have no trouble accepting the idea of the availability of resources from the deeper dimension; in fact, they will tell you of those moments when they have seen through the stubborn covering of the outer like the lifting of a veil. At such times, the outer is transformed by the revelation of the true inner. However, these faith responses must never be regarded as utopian retreats from the world of problems. On the contrary, they are spiritual counterattacks against the brutal challenges of the outer world, daring anyone to move them. Going it on faith is certainly no effortless flight to paradise. To shut out the world of appearance, even for a moment, conjures up the picture of David standing up against Goliath.

If I have learned anything from the spiritual empiricists, it is that we cannot experience a vital faith relationship with God on the basis of someone else's religion. Like "quick studies," we may borrow another's faith ideas, words, and phrases; but this will inevitably be minus the dynamic power present in the original. So we have the depressing spectacle of incredibly potent religious words such as "faith" used in a rather cosmetic sense, when in reality such a vital component is part of God's arsenal of strategic weapons of spiritual warfare that can be used in the crisis battles of life and death. It is pathetic to hear faith relegated almost exclusively to the domestic environment of a church sanctuary or its television counterpart. The tragedy in this is not that we talk about faith in church, but rather that we do not use faith in our everyday lives. Faith by its very nature is an expression denoting action. It is the up-front willingness to act on belief. It is the doer, not the talker. Faith reduced to a dull, rhetorical symbol is an incalculable loss, particularly when we find ourselves in crisis and in need of the strategy of faith.

The spirit of God is ever our contemporary, alive with vibrant possibility, willing to create new applications of faith and recharge old ones. It is such a shame to forfeit firsthand faith experiences with the spirit because we've been neutralized by secondhand theoretical religion. Why not pick up the gauntlet of faith in a time of crisis and let God use those moments, though the air is chilled with uncertainty and the situation unpromising. We might just discover what the pioneers and perfectors of our faith by faith had available to them.

A noteworthy example of someone who lived through a crisis time with extraordinary faith is Julia Ward Howe. Mrs. Howe was a writer, a reform advocate, a lecturer, with a flair for music. In November of 1861, she left the comfort of her Boston home to be with her physician husband in the armed-camp atmosphere of Washington, D.C. He had recently been appointed by President Lincoln to head the sanitary commission of the newly created medical department of the Union Army. She found him working sixteen hours a day, trying to provide sanitary conditions for the military despite poor drinking water, inadequate food, and living conditions that were below minimal standards. Being a man of conscience and professional integrity, it was all he could do to maintain his sanity in that deterioriating environment. Most of the time he was anxious, tense, irritable—indeed, poor company for his wife.

One day Mrs. Howe decided that it was time for him to take a few hours away from his responsibilities. She arranged with a group of friends to go on a picnic out in the country, where he might unwind and enjoy a respite from his duties. They had traveled only a short distance from the city when their brief holiday was interrupted by the sound of marching feet and the clatter of gun carriages coming up behind them. A long blue line of soldiers were soon passing by, many of whom Mrs. Howe observed were "mere boys." As they marched, they sang a lively tune; but the words, by contrast, were anything but inspiring. Written by a Southerner with good intentions, the lyrics told of a certain John Brown whose body eventually lies "a moldering in the grave." Perhaps when first composed, those melancholy words had some special meaning; but that was a long time ago, and now they were dreadfully out of phase. However, the melody was joyously stirring and powerful.

On the return trip some of the picnic crowd, aware of Mrs. Howe's considerable writing talent, began urging her to create some new words to match the beauty of that marching song. Back at their hotel Dr. Howe retired early, but Mrs. Howe could not sleep. Her mind was on all those young men she had seen marching off to war. She could feel the presence of death and destruction hovering about her and for the moment she was swallowed by a crisis of depressing thoughts. For some reason, she began reflecting on the day's experience, particularly that bright melody the soldiers had been trying to sing. She got out of bed, walked across the room and opened the window. What she saw nearly brought her to her knees. Hundreds, perhaps thousands of troops, like legions of dark angels, were passing the hotel and slowly making their way toward the battle area. Out beyond the steady movement of military columns were concentric circles of sentries' watchfires as far as the eye could see.

Deliberately, she closed her eyes; and in a sheer act of faith began to pray—that is, to be open to whatever God might send her to meet the challenge of that crisis moment. Gradually, despite reminders of the harsh reality of war, she began seeing something else. What she had previously observed as the fires of posted sentries had miraculously arranged themselves into the shape of a person that she recognized as the Christ. Incredibly, right there in the midst of that seemingly hopeless, desperate situation, she was seeing her Lord plunged into the crisis of dark human events. Seeing him there was like tapping a wellspring of faith deep within. Words began pushing up through the inner corridors of her being. She grabbed a pencil and paper and excitedly began writing:

> I have seen him in the watchfires of a hundred circling camps; They have builded him an altar in the evening dews and damps; I can read his righteous sentence by the dim and flaring lamps; His day is marching on. Glory! glory! Hallelujah! Glory! glory! Hallelujah! Glory! glory! Hallelujah! His truth is marching on.

That which stimulated the genius of Julia Ward Howe is with each of us at this very moment. It is the presence of the One who is "closer to us than breathing, nearer than hands and feet," who has placed intimations of his being within us that only faith can open, allowing spirit to touch spirit. Mrs. Howe's story is not an Olympian tale for the benefit of us poor mortals here below. This is a self-verifying testimony concerning a spiritual reality, a divine taproot of potentiality that is available to each one of us. The Julia Ward Howe story and others like it are real because they correspond with the experiences of many who have likewise been stimulated through faith. Each episode refers to that which each of us is capable of experiencing in terms of our own circumstances and need.

If you are reading this while suffering a crisis problem that defies every attempt at solution, then let me lead you gently toward the writer of the closing book of the Bible. John, the author of the Book of Revelation, would appear to have written his richly symbolic book with its spiritual allusions and supernatural scenery from an ivory tower a mile high. It seems no one could have written as he did except in the rarified atmosphere of undisturbed spirituality and perfect peace. The fact is, just the opposite is true.

John was a prisoner on the volcanic island of Patmos. He labored in the mines as a slave of the roman emperor. His outer life was ground under by a repressive environment, but he found a way to freedom despite his outer circumstances. He did not find that liberation by escaping to another place or by evasion of harsh reality. Rather, he found another world of surpassing truth right where he was. He explained his discovery in words so triumphant that they might just blow the cobwebs from the corridors of your reluctant faith. He wrote, "I John, your brother . . . was on the island called Patmos. . . . I was in the Spirit . . ." (Rev. 1:9–10). And later he declares, "Behold, the dwelling of God is with men. He will dwell with them, and they shall be his people, and God himself will be with them . . ." (Rev. 21:3). Out of that realization came a living, breathing faith that gave him the transcending power to overcome. Such faith was and is a God-given strategy for crisis times.

Notes

1. William James, *The Varieties of Religious Experience* (New York: Random House, 1902), p. 535. Also see George Sheehan, *Running and Being* (New York: Simon and Shuster, 1978), pp. 202-3.
2. This discussion was inspired in part by Richard Barness, "The Battle Hymn of the Republic," *Liberty Magazine*, July/August 1976, pages 10-11.

CHAPTER 2

The Pathway of the Soul

WHEN IT comes to examining the inner life, most people would just as soon be left alone. Leave all that to the mystics and those that are just naturally religious. A fearless inner inventory is about as inviting as the sound of a dentist's drill. The idea of taking on spiritual disciplines makes the Christian life look like a long series of yokes and crosses, with hard lessons and constant homework.

It is far more pleasant to turn to the outer world, with its multiplicity of preoccupations, than to become a moral/spiritual fitness buff. It is no fun to struggle to know the inner self and, for the purposes of this study, make inquiries within about the soul and the role it has to play in our crisis times. We've done our best to avoid such encounters. Admittedly, we are more outer- than inner-directed. For example, we've become so externally focused that we scarcely notice the blurring of distinctions in the moral/spiritual order. We seem quite indifferent to the subtle shifts in moral value and the quiet supplanting of inner spiritual law. For example, sometime you might take a long look at the way we define words in terms of our bias to the outer-superficial. Have you observed that, within a generation, "lust" has become the "natural urge"? Similarly, "gluttony" is now "eating well"; "wrath" is now "righteous indignation"; "greed" is now "looking out for yourself"; "laziness" is "just taking it easy"; "pride" is now "self-respect"; "blind ambition" is now "getting ahead"; "being nasty" is now "assertiveness"; "honesty" is what *I* do, and "lying" is what *you* do.

But when, in the natural course of events, a crisis comes barreling down on us like a runaway freight train, or a less dramatic reversal of good fortune shakes our comfortable outer world and we are forced to run for cover, where do we go? If we look within, we behold a tragically neglected wasteland, bleak and forbidding. But how could it be otherwise when we have used so much of our vital energies building and expanding the outer life at the expense of the inner experience? The soul, which I define as an inner organism through which spiritual energies are channeled, must be given proper recognition and exercise if it is to fulfill its vital function.

The problem is that we have created first and foremost a life custom-built by addiction to the transitory, which in moments of crisis is like the proverbial house of straw. On the other hand, it could have been different if somewhere along the way we had undertaken some self-scrutiny. We might also have become aware of our inner resources—the health-giving power, the light of God's purifying love, and the redeeming influence of his presence—all transmitted to us through the instrument of the soul.

At this point, I want to put you in touch with the latent

capacity of your soul as a prelude to studying its strategic role in times of crisis. I'll cite some of the obstacles in making this connection and, finally, comment on the unique strategy provided by your soul for crises that inevitably occur in life. Let me try and clear up some of the misconceptions and discrepancies that have become obstacles in discovering this vital spiritual organ. First of all the soul, for many, is a meaningless term. It is acknowledged popularly in the Faustian motif as a commodity sold to the devil. We can eat "soul food," talk about a song that has "soul," or listen to a singer who has "soul." Occasionally, people wonder aloud about their souls going to heaven, and others claim they know all about the soul and its destiny.

As Christians, we have inherited both the Hebrew and Greek ideas concerning the soul. For the Hebrews, the soul and body are one. We are told, "And the Lord God formed man of the dust of the ground, and breathed into his nostrils the breath of life; and man became a living soul" (Gen. 2:7, KJV). The Hebrews make no distinction between the spirit, the soul, and the flesh. All are one. Conversely, the Greeks saw the soul in dualistic opposition to the body. The Greek philosopher Plato spoke of the soul as a prisoner of the body.

To be sure, Christian thinkers have been influenced by both of these views. If the New Testament idea of the soul is carefully examined, while traces of Hebrew and Greek influences are apparent, the overwhelming point of view is that the soul is a life principle. More distinctly, the soul is essentially the real self. Dr. George Buttrick, eminent preacher, teacher, and Bible scholar, used to say, "The real self (the soul) says of all that is found in Christ, 'That is I, if I could become myself.' "[1] So the real self, the high self, is what the soul actually is. The soul, when allowed to operate without encumbrance, is not only capable of putting us in touch with the power that can help us fulfill our highest potentiality but it dignifies our lives by its God-inspired functioning—all of which is essential when facing crisis moments.

What I have just written may not square with what you've been exposed to in church teaching. This is primarily due to the immense influence of the fourth-century church father, St. Augustine. This heralded Christian leader vehemently denied that there is any spiritual quality present in a person's original nature. He taught that we do not have the capacity to choose good. We have no inherent worth. For him, the soul was corrupt, and whatever good would come to a human being would be by divine miracle.

I spent nearly a year working with an alcoholic who early in life had been trained for the Catholic priesthood. In his more morose moments, he would lament in typical Augustinian fashion, "We're all rotten bastards, and Adam is at fault." He was, of course, referring to the church teaching concerning the fall of Adam and the doctrine of original sin. While St. Augustine did not originate this doctrine, nor was he one hundred percent wed to it, he gave it credibility by making it an integral part of his approach to Christian theology. All of us, according to the Augustinian doctrine, are depraved because of our inherited connection with Adam. Reduced to the dull level of literalness Adam and Eve, our primordial parents, disobeyed God and all of their human offspring must forever suffer the consequences of their sin. As the rabbis teach, "In Adam all men sinned," and "In Adam we all died."

Augustine early in life was involved with a sect known as the Manicheans, who taught a mixed bag of Gnostic ideas blended with Persian, Greek, Egyptian, and Christian thought. This philosophy emphasized the hostility between flesh and the spirit. For the Manicheans, the fall of Adam was viewed in the same sense as "the fall" in Plato's *Dialogues*, where the imperial soul of the upper world, failing to nourish its wings with trust, beauty, and goodness, tumbles into the world of flesh and becomes a prisoner in the cave of the physical body. Augustine was decidedly influenced by these teachings. He also read back into the writings of St. Paul a negative estimate of human nature about which Paul was not entirely consistent. You must remember that Paul had been trained as a rabbi and would have respected the traditions of his people, including the Fall and all of its ramifications; but, on occasion, he spoke imaginatively and generously of the soul's potential—which does not make him thoroughgoing one way or the other.

Luther, Calvin, Knox, and other reformers continued in this negative tradition, regarding "the soul" as captive to evil. The main current of Reformation theology maintains that there is an inherent, ingrained wickedness in all persons. We are evil and there is no health in us. We are guilty and under the penalty of sin from the beginning of the race. The soul, which might have been the higher organ of spiritual response, is corrupt. Help can only come from outside ourselves. Theologically, we have the doctrine of atonement, whereby Christ intercedes on our behalf, paying the penalty of our sin by his death on the cross. To the extent that Christ is accepted in this role by faith, the transaction of "he for me" miracle occurs.

As if the soul had not suffered enough from theological detraction, it would be dealt still another blow through the teaching of Sir Isaac Newton, who, until the time of Einstein, gave us our way (at least scientifically) of looking at the world. The implications of Newton's theory applied to all technologies of the time. His mechanical hypothesis of the space-occupying of matter obeying certain unalterable universal laws became the primary pattern of scientific-philosophical thought. For him, the world of matter was completely predictable. There were no hidden mysteries. The big show was the awesome, clocklike movement of the material cosmos. Consequently, the soul's place as a creative, unpredictable presence was by this frame of reference reduced to that of a shrinking shadow.

Much of the theological and scientific negative data regarding the soul should be weighed in the balance of Jesus' teaching. His approach to human nature can in no way be considered shallow or unrealistic. He knew what was in human beings better than anyone who ever lived. He suffered and died by the will of men, yet he believed far more in peoples' divine possibilities than in their satanic predispositions. He never stopped promoting the possibility that anyone might come home to truth, however depraved his or her condition. Frankly, I don't see how the Augustinians of any generation can explain Jesus' parable of the prodigal son, which most Bible scholars maintain was among his most important teachings. Whatever else, the parable is a scorching denial of the depravity doctrine. It makes ridiculous the picture of God as an angry, vindictive deity who must have his sacrificial pound of flesh in order to appease his own wrath against his creatures who disobeyed him.

As you may recall, the prodigal son, defiant and ego-driven, demanded his inheritance. Taking no thought of his responsibility to either his father or brother, he launched on a monumental spree of drinking, whoring, gambling, and wasting in a far country. Eventually he ended up out of money, out of friends, filthy, helpless, and homeless. In desperation, he accepted employment working for a pig farmer who, for wages, allowed the young man to sleep with his pigs and to eat what they ate. One day, according to Jesus, the prodigal, though mired in personal crisis, did some soul-searching—which, as we know, led to a life-changing event. The question is, if the prodigal son was as depraved in spirit as Augustine contended was the general condition of humanity, then how was he capable of responding to the redemptive solution, particularly when it came from within? Without any apparent outside help, including supernatural intervention; without so much as a bath, a change of clothes, or a good meal, the prodigal had a startling moment of clarity in which "he came to himself" and began his journey home (Luke 15:11-32).

This "coming to self" is a crucial event emanating from the sanctuary of a person's soul. This sanctuary does not belong to the world, it is God's. To come to yourself is to find God at home in you. Jesus was describing the pathway of the soul when he described a young man who, while his outer resources were dissipated, was still imprinted deep inside to return to his father.

The influence of the soul in any time of crisis is to get us home to God as quickly as possible—not just in thought or desire, but in fact. That is why, when in trouble, we frequently feel that stabbing sense of naive astonishment—"Why me?"—that may suggest more than self-pity. It might also denote equally the inner dismay that this could be happening to me, equipped as I am with a living soul of God! Jesus' description of God as Father vibrating with forgiving love is anything but a petulant, vindictive patriarch. According to Jesus' story, God the

Father, who has never given up waiting for his errant son, at last sees him a long way off and runs to meet him, hugging him around the neck and tenderly kissing him. There are two confessions in this parable. In the first instance, the prodigal rehearses a speech out of fear. This is the external self, quivering in anxiety and despair. "Father, I have sinned against heaven and before you; I am no longer worthy to be called your son; treat me as one of your hired servants" (Luke 15:18-19). The second confession is from the soul. The words are the same, but the accent is entirely different. The soul knows to whom it belongs. The second confession is not out of despair, it is from love, repentant—turning, faithing, love muffled in a divine embrace.

At the heart of the parable, the soul's purpose is revealed as that of restoring us to our true relationship with God. This relationship is to be complete without contingency. No matter how far removed we think we are from him, he has planted something in us that Augustine (in one of his more devotional rather than dogmatic moments) allowed, "Our hearts are restless until they rest in thee."[2] Why? Because at center we are God's and are constructed to experience him, and no doctrine of depravity or belittling scientific rationale can alter the fact that God is ever our contemporary through the divine identification in our souls.

If you are in a crisis, hemmed in by the onslaught of external events, feeling weak and powerless, I want you just for a moment to consider that, while you're suffering the pressure from outer events, you may be undercut even more destructively by an insidious spiritual inferiority complex brought on by the negative theological influences I've been describing. Right now a damning self-estimate may be crippling your soul's transmission facility to prevail in response to your current crisis. I don't know how many times I've sent people in trouble to a church sanctuary to be alone and almost always they look at me blankly as though to ask, "Be alone with what?" Some time ago, the columnist Walter Kerr wrote about the great composer Jerome Kern. He said there were times when Kern would leave the theater where one of his musical compositions was in rehearsal, and would find a smaller room with a piano where he could be alone. There he would sit down and pick out the show tune with one finger. "So what was he doing," Mr. Kerr asked, "Abandoning all that orchestral lushness for so small a sound? He was trying to find out if the naked melody had enough strength to stand on its own."[3]

This is the question that can't be answered until the soul is stretched beyond its negative conditioning and self-imposed limitation. You may go to church and be told that Jesus saves your soul; but from all you've been taught, either consciously or unconsciously, you may be wondering if your soul is even there, let alone worth saving. Day and night we are tutored by a culture that tells us we are basically animal-like or that we are unimportant cogs in the machinery of a vast impersonal universe. At worst, we have been likened to a "parasite infesting the epidermis of a runt among the planets." Thank God for William Shakespeare, who has never stopped giving sage advice: "Self-love my liege is not so vile a sin as self-neglecting"[4]—particularly when that self is the inner presence, the soul capable of making a creative naked melody supplied by God.

Let the profound words of a brilliant surgeon, Dr. Wilder Penfield, seep into your consciousness. Dr. Penfield was reflecting on the two streams of awareness observable when a person is lying on an operating table.

One has to do with past memory, the other present experience. He says, "There is something more that we come here to consider and cannot even name. There is something more that is able to see, and reflect, and compare such things as two streams of awareness. I am not expressing this very well but I am sure you guess what I am driving at. There is something more than just the stream of awareness.... There is something that looks out of the eyes of an individual. It changes through the years. It is what the biographer must make his readers familiar with. There is something beyond the stream of conscious experience that we still aren't either naming or identifying or understanding."[5]

The soul as a "definite something" is shrouded, if not by ignorance and confusion, then by mystery. Theology, despite its pretentions, can't explain it any more than general science can explain the workings of the biological organism. One of the foremost scientists in the field of biology, Dr. Lewis Thomas, frankly admits, "We are ignorant about how we work.... Only two centuries ago we could explain everything about everything out of pure reason, and now most of that elaborate and harmonious structure has come apart before our eyes. We are dumb."[6]

But dumb isn't all that bad, if by making such an admission we divest ourselves of preconceived notions and defensiveness about our esteemed opinions and get on with the research that I am encouraging—that is, exploration into the soul. Earlier, we examined a bit of the background and some of the problems in understanding what the soul is. For purposes of further definition, please note that the "soul" is the English translation of the Latin *anima*, which is translated into the Greek as *psyche* and comes back to the English as "mind." For many, the soul and mind are synonymous; and since the soul is the less popular of the two, the mind has eclipsed it in contemporary usage.

However, British psychiatrist E. B. Strauss insists on making a distinction between the soul and the psyche, or mind. He states,

> It is important to assert from the start that the psyche with which the medical psychologist deals is conceptually different from the soul as defined by the theologian. By the psyche we mean the sum total of what we experience both actually and potentially—actual experience constituting the conscious, latent and potential experience the unconscious.... The soul of theology is conceived of in terms of a different kind of discipline. The soul is that part of a man which is unique, individually created, endowed with survival value. It perceives true and real values ... is modified by values, and transformed by Grace.[7]

Strauss holds that the soul is a theological concept understandable only in theological and ontological terms, whereas psyche is to be understood in a psychological frame of reference.

Dr. Strauss is maintaining a position that Jesus advocated, in that there are eternal values that flow out of the deeper or higher dimension of our lives. If we are able to get behind and beneath the shams and deceits of our outer natures and discover to whom we essentially belong and what our real destiny is, a whole new life is made available to us. We discover that our basic nature is not as flesh-oriented as the external mind would have us think. We are, deep down, spirit enabled by the transforming power of Christ to be about the reconstruction of our lives through the enlargement of our soul's capacity to receive all that God has for us.

Contemporary philosopher Ludwig Klages sees the

soul as the meaning or the point of the body's existence. He sees the soul operating spontaneously, naturally, uncontrived, without affection. The soul in polarity, tandem with the body, rides out the cycles, rhythms, and movements of life with unified purpose. However, according to Klages, the psyche or mind is the disrupter of the flow. The mind is always seeking to systematize and formulate, make hard and fast rules, and construct a permanent form. I'm not sure that Klages has helped us to better understand the function of the soul, but he has identified what may be a chief troublemaker.

We are victimized more than we realize by the tyranny of our mental-sensory appetite that feeds on the unstable, often vacillating world of appearance. We keep going home to the wrong place. Our minds are always searching for validating externals that don't validate anymore. We desire some absolute criteria and authority, some arbitrary rule of the outer to make us feel better, when none really exist. So here is the point—once again, the soul is an inner organism through which the spiritual energies enter our being without consultation from the outer environment and remain untransmitted into our experience unless we begin recognizing and experiencing this vital capacity. The energies of the divine realm channelled through the soul make resources available to us that are more powerful and worthy of trust than anything dictated or explained by the appearance level.

Now let us consider on a practical level the release of soul power as a strategic weapon in our arsenal for times of crisis. I want to record a crisis experience in which the energies of my soul played an indispensable role. Some time ago, I was on board an airplane that was to make a routine flight. Flying time to our destination was to take no longer than forty-five minutes. I leaned back and closed my eyes to take a quick nap. An hour and a half later we were still in the air. I began wondering why it was taking so long. My question was soon answered when our pilot came on the intercom to make a startling announcement. He warned us of the distinct possibility that our plane might crash in the next few minutes.

With all the professional objectivity he could muster, he explained that he had been circling Evansville, Indiana, for the past forty-five minutes because the plane was losing hydraulic brake fluid and he wasn't sure that there was enough of that precious fluid to hold the brakes and allow for a safe landing. Simply put, when we hit the ground and he hit the brakes we might just keep going beyond the runway to no one knew where. "So that is why," he pointed out, "all emergency vehicles—ambulances, fire trucks, radio and TV vans are gathering below." I looked out of the window and, sure enough, the airport scene resembled a Hollywood set from an air disaster movie.

Riding an airplane that might crash on landing still seemed totally unreal, until the pilot and stewardesses began giving us emergency instructions. We were asked to remove our glasses, lay aside any sharp objects, and make sure that everything around us was secured. Pillows were passed to each passenger. We were told how to huddle over the pillow for protection. Seat belts were double-checked to make sure they were locked in place.

Ordinarily, I would have been coming apart at the seams in the face of such an apparent crisis. But from the unfamiliar depth of my soul I knew there was another way of responding to this experience, if I could just find the courage and concentration to make a choice. I forced myself to think the most perfect thoughts I could call to mind and those thoughts turned almost instinctively to

Jesus. At first it was impossible to concentrate fully on anything. My mind was like a squirrel cage, racing about with all sorts of panic thoughts. Gradually, I began to be in touch with what I perceived to be Christ's presence. It came as recognizing that something in me could be in close touch with him—and that something was my soul. I discovered in those moments above the airport at Evansville, Indiana, that the soul is the conductor of energy and the vehicle of realizing the power and presence of God.

I must confess that, prior to this crisis, the muscles of my soul were sluggish from disuse; but somehow I was able to call them into action in this demanding moment. Though it sounds strange, those seconds when my soul was working at its optimum, my life on the physical plane and the life to come were one and the same. Whether I occupied space in this dimension or another became insignificant. Then I felt a jolt. The wheels of the plane had touched the ground. We were rolling. Would we stop? Again, I had that feeling of knowing not that we would or wouldn't crash, but that all was in God's hands. I felt totally in tune with the words from the 139th Psalm: "Whither shall I go from thy spirit? Or whither shall I flee from thy presence? If I ascend to heaven, thou art there! If I make my bed in Sheol, thou art there. If I take the wings of the morning and dwell in the uttermost part of the sea, even there thy hand shall lead me and thy right hand shall hold me." I drew on the truth of those words, not exactly mentally, not exactly emotionally, not exactly physically, but in the soul, in the depth part of me. In fact, in that short space of time between touching the ground and coming to a stop I felt spiritual kinship with the great Indian Chief Crazy Horse, who said, "Today is a good day to die." Suffice it to say we landed safely. The plane did take an unusually long time to come to a stop, but thank God the brakes held sufficiently to bring us home safe and sound. It had been a close call in one sense, but the transforming experience accompanying the crisis-event was worth all the tension and anxiety.

If the soul is to be taken seriously, its presence must not only be rediscovered, but freed of its accumulated misinterpretations. I recognize the soul to be the hidden higher self. It is an organ of consciousness capable of tuning us to the Kingdom of God—that is, the higher or God consciousness. The soul as higher self is able to inspire our total being. The soul is not "holy other"; rather, it is like a seed. Quaker Robert Barclay described it as lying in the heart "naked as a grain on the stone ground."[8] It is a gift from God that must be discovered, realized, and experienced.

The soul must become less an object of curiosity, and more a living phenomenon to be seriously cultivated. Of course, the soul is not an infallible witness to all that God has to communicate. The soul transmits to the limit of its particular level of development. Oliver Wendell Holmes' vision of the chambered nautilus moving each year into a house or larger dimension is a picture of the soul in growth. He visualized the soul developing in response to its progress toward God.

> Build thee more stately mansions, O my soul,
> As the swift seasons roll;
> Leave thy low vaulted past,
> Let each new temple nobler than the last,
> Shut thee from heaven with a dome more vast
> Til thou at last art free,
> Leaving thine outgrown shell
> By life's unresting sea.[9]

Let me repeat: discovering the inner or soul life does not immediately transform you into a perfect instrument of communication from within. Your limitations are still present. Your personality traits are still with you. What happens is not the erasing of all that you are, but the heightening of the best that you can be. In practical terms, you may find yourself living from another perspective entirely. As Boris Pasternak would have it, one day you will no longer be saying the opposite of what you feel, nor groveling before what you dislike, nor rejoicing in what brings you nothing but misfortune.

This is where Christ comes into the picture. St. Paul spoke of being in travail until Christ was born in his followers. Christ born in us is the transformation of the mind of the flesh into the mind or soul that was in Christ Jesus. This is the process through which the highest energies, clarified insights, sharpened sensitivities, quickened aspirations, currents of love can be realized. Christ operating in us and through us exercises the full potential of our souls. Our soul, so stimulated and allowed to function as it was intended, can channel God's guidance, which flows in from a higher realm. In other words, the soul is an instrument of God through which he can help us meet our crisis need.

This is what we need in crisis times. To know that our soul has this capability and to know equally that Christ can operate in us through this inner self. We are, most of us, half crushed by the world's problems but we're also weary of our inner ineptitude. But the simple fact is that we have been splendidly equipped for this life, and the soul is part of our equipment. There is a memorable exchange in the Old Testament when King David on his death bed commissioned his son Solomon to build the temple in Jerusalem. King David said, "... Be strong, and of good courage, and do it" (Chron. 28:20). The soul has the "do-it" capacity.

If you're really serious about this growth process, the renewing and restoration of your soul to a fully participating organ of higher consciousness, then let me reinforce your dedication. We do belong to the higher order. We are citizens of the Kingdom of God with a spiritual passport stamped with the image of our maker. When St. Paul was preaching to the people of Lycaonia he said, "God has not left himself without witness" (Acts 14:17). The soul, in fact, is that witness, with its own unique testimony to present. And though it may be hidden beneath the subsoil of all our superficial ideas, attitudes, and crowd-level thinking, the soul is in essence what we really are as living beings whose core point is in connection with God.

It was the church father Tertullian who, in his *De Testimonio Aninae*, made an unusually difficult demand on his own soul. Perhaps he was weary of rumor, lofty testimony, and logical inference concerning the existence of this inner spiritual organ. He wrote,

> Stand forth O soul ... from whatever source, and in whatever way, thou makest man a rational being, in the highest degree capable of thought and knowledge—stand forth and give thy witness. I call thee not as, when fashioned in schools, trained in libraries, fed up in attic academies and porticoes, thou belchest forth wisdom. I address thee, simple and rude, uncultured and untaught, such as they have thee who have thee only; that very thing pure and entire, of road, the street, the workshop. I want thy experience.... Whenever the soul comes to itself, as out of a surfeit, or a sleep, or a sickness, and attains something of its natural soundness, it speaks of God. There is not a soul of man that does not, from the light that is in itself, proclaim God.[10]

Notes

1. George Buttrick, in *The Interpreter's Bible* (Nashville: Abingdon, 1951), vol. 7, p. 456.
2. Augustine, *The Confessions of St. Augustine*, book I, chapter 1.
3. Walter Kerr, in *The New York Times*, January 21, 1980, section 2, p. 5.
4. William Shakespeare, *King Henry the Fifth*, act 2, sc. 4, line 74.
5. John C. Eccles, *Brain and Conscious Experience* (New York: Springer-Verlag, 1963), p. 546.
6. Lewis Thomas, *The Medusa and the Snail* (New York: Viking-Penguin, 1979), p. 145.
7. Victor White, *Soul and Psyche* (New York: Harper & Brothers, 1960), p. 16.
8. Rufus Jones, *Social Law in the Spiritual World* (Philadelphia: Winston, 1904), p. 168.
9. Oliver Wendell Holmes, "The Chambered Nautilus," *The World's Great Religious Poetry*, ed. Caroline Miles Hill (New York: Macmillan, 1938).
10. Rufus M. Jones, *The Testimony of the Soul* (New York: Macmillan, 1937), p. 6.

CHAPTER 3

The Pathway
of the Kingdom

IN JESUS' day it was the custom for a Roman soldier to force anyone he met on the road to carry his military gear. However, there was one stipulation: the person would have to carry it no further than a mile, as marked out on the Roman roads by milestones. Jesus saw the religion of his time cluttered by the same sort of slavish rules. Most people who practiced religion in Jesus' day carried a spiritual pedometer so as to do just what was required of them and no more. By contrast, the religion of Jesus went beyond compulsiveness to law. There was and is no one-mile limit. For Jesus, religion has no joy in it until you have gone the second or the third or however many miles.

In her time of crisis, as noted in a previous chapter, Julia Ward Howe's religion might have gotten her to a window to see a world going to war, but something else helped her to go farther and deeper. She prayed inwardly, looked inwardly, and then saw inwardly another world. And the surprise, the joy, and the power of it are in those words that we love to sing: "In the beauty of the lilies Christ was born across the sea, with a glory in his bosom that transfigures you and me...." Mind you, this was written in a crisis time.

Most people never get to the transfiguring stage because they never get beyond the legalism of religion. For them, the whole thing is a keeping of laws, or the keeping of religious convention. There is a plethora of "party manner" Christianity that has a specific vocabulary, an exclusive group tone, a particular form of worship, and various religious emphases. I have no doubt that religion of this type gets one to the milepost, but it doesn't transfigure one, nor does it give sustaining power in crisis times.

One of the most dramatic spiritual crises recorded in the Bible is the meeting between Jesus and Nicodemus described in the Gospel according to St. John. Basically, this is a meeting of a religious miler and a spiritual marathoner. It must be clearly understood that Nicodemus was a pious Jew, an honored Pharisee, a scupulous keeper of the religious law. He was a ruler of the Jews, which means that he was lay leader of a local synagogue. Some scholars believe he was a teacher, honored and esteemed among his people.

Nicodemus came to Jesus by night, no doubt to examine him out of the glare of the public eye. He began with flattery—which was, and to an extent still is, the oriental way of greeting. But his was more than flattery. Nicodemus was not just complimenting Jesus, he was revealing himself. His emphasis was on the observable things that Jesus had been doing. "Rabbi," he said to Jesus, "we know that you are a teacher come from God; for no one can do these signs [miracles] that you do unless God is with him" (John 3:2).

Note the criterion by which Nicodemus made his value judgment concerning Jesus. He must be a teacher come from God, reasoned Nicodemus, because he could perform mighty deeds. He was doing miraculous things that Nicodemus could see with his eyes. On that basis, Nicodemus determined Jesus' worth. Anyone who could do such sublime acts of power must have come from God.

But suddenly, Jesus answers a question Nicodemus did not ask, concerning Nicodemus' basic relationship with God—a relationship that had nothing to do with keeping rules and regulations or holding high religious office or even signs and wonders. The answer to the question not asked must have shaken Nicodemus to the core. It is a pity that Jesus' words, so powerful and profound, must be seen through the filters of translation. "Verily, verily, Amen, Amen," he thundered in Aramaic. It's difficult to think of an equivalent English expression to match the impact of that ancient attention grabber. It would almost be like the TV newsbreak, "We interrupt our regular programming to bring you this special announcement." Then he spoke lightning-like syllables sparked with the electric pulsations of the Spirit. "I say to you, unless one is born from above he cannot see the Kingdom of God."

You will note that I have substituted "born from above" in place of the more popular translation "born again," or even "born anew." I believe "born from above" or even better "generated from above" is the better translation from the Greek. Nearly all translators acknowledge the legitimacy of this translation. At any rate, Nicodemus was befuddled. He exclaimed, "How can a man be born when he is old? Can he enter a second time into his mother's womb and be born?" (John 3:4).

The starting point of Nicodemus' religious thinking

THE PATHWAY OF THE KINGDOM 39

had always been on the physical level, that is, reinforced by outward experience. That's what the Jewish law seemed to be about—complying with outward rules and legalisms. In fact, that is what religion tends to be in many places, an outward response to outward regulation. So the concept of God is reduced to the image of a judicial authority. Keeping the bare dictates of the law is next to Godliness. You may continue to cling to your prejudices, your illusions, your hang-ups, even your self-justifications—all are allowed as long as you keep the outward law.

In his statement to Nicodemus, Jesus speaks of actually seeing the Kingdom of God and then entering it. The fact is, Jesus spent a considerable part of his ministry instructing people about this kingdom. His parables are filled with allusions to it. He implored people to "seek first the Kingdom." He believed it had already begun, that it was here right now. However, as you read the New Testament, a clear understanding of the Kingdom becomes complicated because of several possible interpretations. In one sense, you get the impression that the Kingdom will come at the end of the age when God will reign in triumph with all of his saints. A second vision is that the Kingdom of God is present in the life of the church that is engaged in warfare against the Kingdom of Evil. Another view has the Kingdom of God as the union of all churches into one super-church. A fourth interpretation is that the Kingdom of God is the consummation that is the goal of human history. Still another more popular impression of the Kingdom of God is that it is the coming of a social order where people the world over will be blessed with peace and plenty.

Any or all of these visions of the Kingdom may be correct; but what I want to examine is what the Kingdom of

God meant to Jesus at the time he was talking to Nicodemus and what its strategic possibilities might be for us in crisis situations. It is reported that some Pharisees demanded that Jesus tell them when the Kingdom of God was coming, even though Jesus previously declared it was at hand. What they were seeking was an outward proof by external signs. Jesus' answer is significant: he says the Kingdom will not come by observation—as though one could say, "Look, here it is," or "There it is"—for "The Kingdom of God is inside you" (Luke 17:21, PHILLIPS).

This is a mind-boggling answer to someone whose world is exclusively bounded by the five senses. The Kingdom of God, according to Jesus, appears to be a higher dimension that can only be experienced as we are empowered or generated from that level. Many theologians, when confronted with these words, refuse to accept it as such; or they change the translation to read that the Kingdom is in the "midst" of you or "among you," or they say that it is a complete mystery. Apparently, they have no vision of a transcendent consciousness.

Jesus' strategy was to reorient Nicodemus, to take him to another starting line for a new race to be run by a new Nicodemus. Jesus was not asking Nicodemus to change his theology or to accept a new creed, or to join a new church. Would that it were that simple. He didn't want a recycled Nicodemus. Jesus insisted, "Unless one is born of water and the spirit he cannot enter the Kingdom of God" (John 3:5).

Professor Edmund Perry has explained that, in the original Greek, the correct reading should be, "You must be born out of your mother's water and you must be born out of the human spirit."[1] But if you are to experience the Kingdom of God it cannot be done while immersed in fetal waters and joined to the sensual environment. "That which is born of the flesh," continued Jesus, "is flesh. And that which is born of Spirit is spirit. Do not marvel that I said to you, You must be generated from above. The wind blows where it will and you hear the sound of it, but you do not know whence it comes or whither it goes; so it is with every one who is born of the Spirit" (John 3:6–8). Jesus is not speaking of a random outpouring of spirit. This is not some kind of bizarre phenomenon designed to excite a crowd of enthusiasts. The wind of the spirit is not capricious. It does not transcend the objectives of God. It is not outside God's purpose.

Poor Nicodemus! He had been plunged into a crisis that resulted from being challenged by the faith strategies of Christ. Here was a man who had prided himself on his religious development. His total commitment and devotion to every jot and tittle of the religious law was his most cherished lifetime accomplishment. He was a religious professional. He knew exactly how many doves were needed to be sacrificed for such and such a blessing. He was honored as an authority on the proper worship of God. And now he was being told by this young Galilean prophet that there was a whole dimension of spiritual reality available to him about which he had no knowledge and into which he would never enter as long as he remained locked into his present level of development, which included being a leading religious authority.

Imagine yourself in such a position. Think of yourself as a religious celebrity, widely quoted and praised. Perhaps you appear regularly on television or radio. You may have a syndicated column in newspapers appearing across the country. Thousands are attracted to your speaking talent, your powerful intellect, your ability to persuade. You may have the esteem of your peers and the love of your faithful devotees. Then one evening you are confronted by the human face of God challenging your priorities—not equivocating, not pleading, but declaring from the foundation of life itself that you must be generated from above if you are to experience his Kingdom. Above all else, this requires that you deny yourself, give up all your pretensions and self-merit. That you give up your illusions of what you think is important; that you give yourself over to life lived from a higher level, no longer determined by the old value systems. You must become a changed person—born from another dimension. You must become a new person, God's person. Then and only then, particularly as a religious person, will you know what you're talking about and living from. Talk about promoting an existential crisis!

I have seen the transformation that Jesus precipitated in the life of Nicodemus happen to other people as well. I have witnessed the transformation of a twenty-six-year-old man indulging himself in a life of alcoholism and drug abuse literally stop in his tracks and give up the old life, beginning with his immature sorrows and disappointments and finally the sins he had hugged so close for so long. I saw him cast away his rationalizations and phony pretensions. Finally, writhing in shame, he humbled himself and gave himself totally to Christ. One day I saw him coming to me, his face bathed in tears, his clothes wet from walking in the rain. He told me he had seen it, a landscape deeper and more beautiful than anything he had ever imagined. He had seen the Kingdom of God from the parking lot of our church.

I saw it happen with a forty-year-old accountant who was facing the crisis of spiritual integrity. He had joined the church, was being drawn into the deeper fellowship, was attending a Bible study prayer group, but was still doing business with a crime boss at a handsome salary. Then, on one of those mornings in the businessmen's prayer group, he faced the professional crisis with Christ. He made his decision. He quit the job paying him the big money because he had seen the vision of a richer economy. He had seen the Kingdom and there was no lack of employment in legitimate occupations in that realm.

I saw it happen with a brilliant young executive working for a giant corporation. He was being groomed for no less than the presidency of this national company, but he was a Christian. He decided he could not stop being a Christian Monday through Friday. He decided to institute early-morning Bible study prayer groups for employees who wished to attend before work. He was severely reprimanded for instigating such an activity. He was told it was unhealthy for the morale of the total work force. While faced with the crisis of what to do, he told me that he could not deny his Lord over a hundred and fifty thousand dollar a year salary and the presidency of that corporation—not after he had seen the glory of the Kingdom of God. So he resigned to take his talents to another place of business where he would not be compromised.

I saw it happen with a young woman who was so much like Mary of Magdalene. She was a church member, married with children, but now and then her old life of cheap thrills, alcohol, sex, and violence would reassert itself. Though she had become a Christian and was attending a prayer group, she would return to her former haunts and relive the past. After several months of living under holy orders, she decided one evening "to do some partying." Incredibly, she phoned to announce her intention. I asked her to meet me in the church sanctuary. There, after much prayer through the agony of confessing tears, she washed away the need for low-level diversion. But, more important, the outpouring of her pent-up guilt and shame was like crucifying the old self. And what came in its place was someone born into the Kingdom of God.

I saw it happen with the woman who was determined to kill herself because she found so little within worth living for. Periodically, overdosing was for her a way to cope. She had attended a variety of churches, visited with several counselors, and then she tried a prayer group. There she met people who loved her for no other reason than what she could be in Christ. It has been a long and weary road, with several crises along the way. But slowly she is discovering the grandeur of the inner Kingdom that is worth loving. Most of all, she is becoming aware of the Lord who sees her as she really is beyond sentiment and emotion through the eyes of redeeming love.

The Kingdom of God does not just happen to people. We have our work to do. As we grow into a clarity of vision about a life beyond yet resident in our flesh, we may be misunderstood by others, perhaps ridiculed. Over a hundred years ago, Robert Browning wrote a poem that the literary critics of the time ridiculed. The title was "Pippa Passes." It was about an orphan girl, named Pippa, who worked long hours in a mill and had just one holiday a year. On that particular day she walked out into the early dawn to observe the splendor of nature.

> The year's at spring
> And day's at the morn;
> Morning's at seven;
> The hillside's dew-pearled;
> The lark's on the wing;
> The snail's on the thorn:
> God's in his heaven—
> All's right with the world!

Perhaps it was not the best poetry in the world, or even the best theology—but what the cynical world did not realize, according to the late William Lyons Phelps of Yale, was that Browning was recording a crisis tragedy in the life of that little girl. It seems that the night previous to her holiday she had witnessed a murder in the factory resulting from a chain of evil events. Still in a state of shock, she turned to the things she knew best in the natural environment that would help her get her bearings and put her back in touch with the deeper realities. There she saw a lark on the wing, where larks are supposed to be. She saw a snail on a thorn, where snails are known to be. She saw the coming of spring in perfect order, the clear, bright beginning of a new day, and a hillside with the look of perfection. Finally, she was able to declare from the depth of her being that with everything in its place and God in His heaven, all was right with the world—despite the crisis events of the previous day. Seeing into the Kingdom, she could live on the basis of that inner revelation.

But how does it happen? How can I become a Kingdom person knowing in my honest moments how weak I am; knowing my petty low-level living; my irritability; my meanness, resentment, envy, vanity, egoism; knowing my prejudices and selfishness and shoddy motives? How do I get from where I am to where I would be if I could? It seems so impossible, particularly in this day and age. You may have to forgive me for using the following example, but it seems fit. Consider the prehistoric Cro-Magnon race. Twenty thousand years ago, they lived in a world so filled with danger and violence that it is difficult to believe that anyone or anything could have survived. Everything was tempest-tossed and in turmoil. There was cataclysmic movement of glaciers, huge, ferocious animals prowled about, disease was rampant, and always there was the daily ordeal of finding food and water. Each day the Cro-Magnons faced immutable life-and-death crisis. How could they do anything else but spend all their waking hours just eking out an existence?

Archeologists have discovered that there was at least one Cro-Magnon who, despite his or her inhospitable environment, one day became an artist. Somehow, some way, this person—very slowly and by the light of a sputtering torch—began to paint a familiar animal. The artist painted a bison, and it is a marvel. There is nothing crude about this art. Incredible as it may seem, a subhuman living in crisis times executed poignant art in accurate color and marvelous proportion. The painting is done with rare detail—even, I might add, spiritual sensitivity. And it was painted on the ceiling of the artist's cave.

What caused this ancient artist to separate himself from his group, tribe, and clan and do something totally different? I hazard to guess what motivated the Cro-Magnon. Perhaps he or she pushed open some inner door of primitive consciousness and for a split second saw into the Kingdom, and was helped to the next evolutionary step that was part of God's plan.

In physical birth, we have no choice when we shall be born. At some point in the term of our mother's pregnancy we are pushed into this life. In spiritual life, no such push is given. Rather, we have to make a choice. We must begin with the ultimate premise that God and I—the *real* I—are not separate: we are one. If we are to experience this oneness, which is Kingdom living, we must by a force of will open as many windows, roofs—knock down as many walls of our private lives in as many areas as we can that our relationship with God will be one of no separation. This is the preliminary action for the spiritual birth to occur. You can live as near to God as did Nicodemus in an esteemed religious order of Bibles, devotional books, theological tracts, service to the church, worship services, and Sunday School attendance records, but still you might not find him. God may be as close as breathing, nearer than hands and feet, but only those who consciously attempt to connect with him in thought, action, temperament, and being will experience birth into His Kingdom.

When does generation from above take place? Often it happens in times of crisis and tribulation, when your external world is in big trouble and the old ways of handling a problem aren't working. Sometimes these rough and painful experiences are openings to divine inflow. It is interesting to read through the various periods of history and note how often, despite the worst of times, spiritual growth and development occurred. Historian William Lecky, in his *History of European Morals*, wrote, "There probably has never existed upon earth a community whose members were bound to one another by a deeper or purer affection than the Christians in the days of the persecutions."[2]

Perhaps right now, in a moment of personal ordeal, you're discovering that what may have helped you in the past is no longer effective. May I suggest a new way of dealing with your problems? This may sound radical, but if you are willing to admit that the old natural you is not equal to the task of the present crisis, you may be ready to seek for what is known in the spiritual life as a new birth. Let me urge you to take this seriously, because the birth of a new you born into and through your life will be perfectly able to cope with all the problems that you are now facing with transforming power. I would not presume to define the parameters of this birth, I'm not sure that it can be reduced to precise language or detailed specifications; but it does happen by the power of the Spirit. Like a child safely held in the arms of his mother after birth, so after a spiritual birth we have a similar sense of being loved and belonging. We are being changed by that to which we've been opening ourselves. We haven't got all the answers, but at least the metamorphosis has begun, and this is the way of God.

Jesus says to everyone seeking to overcome some particular problem in their lives that they must live from that which is generated from above manifesting itself from within. To live from such a perspective requires repentence. When I speak of repentence I am not referring to an expression of being regretful. Regret and repent do not mean the same thing. The Greek word *metanoia* translated into the English as "repentence" means to "change your mind." It also signifies "to turn around in mind." In Acts 3:19, *metanoia* and "to be turned" are put together. This idea comes from the Greek horsemen who would wheel their horses around; this, in Christian terminology, is defined as "to repent and be turned." Changing our mind, turning in a new direction, signifies that we have a choice. We can "stop the world" even in crisis and observe our customary way of response. We do not have to be slaves to the sensory way of thinking. We have another system of response available, indeed another life.

The Kingdom of God that Jesus taught is different than anything on earth. It operates by another authority. Therefore, the Kingdom of God person has more options than anyone else. If you know such people you're aware of how little public opinion means to them. In fact, what seems to be crisis to you is not crisis to these people, because their audience is God and God alone. So, in this sense, even crisis itself is redefined. If you compliment these people they are likely to hang their heads and say very little. They never consider that what they've done is good or praiseworthy. They are not very high on how the public perceives them. They know how faulty such perceptions can be, and how such reasoning leads to misconception, self-centeredness, superiority, conceit, and arrogance. In all, these people seem to be constantly shifting their lives to an inner basis of perception. They are going about the important discipline of evolving spiritually, which means they are going about their daily lives attempting to stay awake, making deeper observations into their own activities, opening their eyes to the need of others, enlarging their outlook, deepening their moral consciousness, and doing their work in the world more effectively. They realize that God has made himself available to them in ways so fantastic that even in crisis times they are not without God's leading. In fact, crisis experience opens their lives as a theater to the glory of God.

Fortunately or unfortunately, the most amazing thing about growth in this dimension is that you can't draw up any set of specifications to cover the implications of living from the Kingdom of God. No creed can describe it. No collection of theological words, however brilliant, can express it. The sense of this new life goes beyond the logic and rhetoric mills. It can't even be taught as such. Each of us receives on our own level. Jesus continually said that the Kingdom of God is like *something*. And that "like something" depends on your growth in spirit and your willingness to keep turning and evolving toward more understanding.

If you are to be generated from above, you must rid yourself of the divided mind. This is the mind that vacillates between the higher and the lower levels. We often experience a directional wobble in a crisis situation. The answer to the divided mind is a "single eye" concentrated on Jesus. If Jesus is carefully read, reflected on, and received, he can give you the Kingdom of God. In fact, he is the embodiment of it. But Jesus cannot be, so to speak, poured into the life of anyone. The experience of being generated from above does not just happen. There is a strategy involved in this venture. Jesus is the supreme witness in history of a person passing through various initiations that helped to develop the spiritual powers that were resident in him.

If you're intrigued with this sort of life, then examine the testimony of St. Paul. Paul was a hard-headed Pharisee, a one time Jewish vigilante, self-confessed persecutor of Christians. It would appear that he was once a religious fanatic with a true-believer mentality, a belligerent anti-Christian. Rounding up Christians for execution was to him a sport—that is, until he met Jesus in an unusual crisis moment on the road to Damascus. Not a Jesus out there, as some would believe, but a Jesus of his inner life. Later, recalling that incident, he explained, "It pleased God ... to reveal his son in me" (Gal. 1:15–16).

Jesus was revealed to St. Paul from the Kingdom level. But how could an avowed hater of the Christians have such an experience? How could he have heard the voice of Jesus speaking to either his inside or outside being? Of this we are not told. My guess is he may have been having an "existential crisis"; or, as they say in Alcoholics Anonymous, he might have been doing a "fearless moral inventory," becoming aware that his vendetta against the Christians was ill-advised and counterproductive. Maybe he realized that his real sensitivities were being strangled by the fungus of a sick prejudice and that he would have much preferred a free and open conscience to God than be extolled among the Jews as their number one hatchet man. In this crisis struggle between his high and low self came a moment of truth. Suddenly he was ready to listen and the voice of Jesus was heard.

Later, Paul would write to the church of Galatia, "I bear in my body the marks of the Lord Jesus" (Gal. 6:17). The obvious interpretation of those words would have to do with his physical suffering in the cause of Christ. His human body did bear the scars of beating, stonings, pummellings, and foul play of every kind. Without subtracting one degree of respect for Paul's physical suffering for his Lord, could not the scars also refer to the marks of his new birth when the old man Saul wrestled with the new man Paul in a titanic crisis battle of the outer versus the inner? For most of us, the battle lines between life in the world and Kingdom life may be far removed from our present thought. But, with Paul, this was an ever-present crisis struggle.

When personal crisis comes, it is well to note who is doing what. Notice that it is our outer person who is always fuming and fussing. It is the external me who can see nothing but the most narrow and despairing meaning in the challenge experience. It is the surface person who is rolled over by the inexorable events of the appearance level, and what is extraordinary is that we always refer to the "panicky outer self" as *I* or *me*, as though there were no other I or me. Invariably, when crises come, it is the little outer self with which we are attempting to cope.

Paul knew this only too well. Consequently, he set out to enhance and affirm his inner being. He saw in Christ the means to that end. He knew that "if anyone is in

Christ, he is a new creation" (2 Cor. 5:17). A new creation is generated by the power from on high. This new inner person is a living product—is, in fact, an emissary of the Kingdom of God. But if this new person is to grow and prosper, a daily dying to the outer sense-oriented self is required. That outer preoccupation must be replaced by a life directed toward God. Paul would say, "I have been crucified with Christ; it is no longer I who live, but Christ who lives in me; and the life I now live in the flesh I live by faith in the Son of God" (Gal. 2:20). This new "I" can cope because it channels and is sustained by the Kingdom of God power, which is uniquely gifted to deal with outer crisis.

In that grand declaration, "it is no longer I who lives, but Christ who lives in me," Paul states categorically that his inner person is in reality the Christ. The life that pours into our souls from the Kingdom of God is the Spirit of the risen Christ whose triumphant life would work through us despite our weakness during crisis times. Is this just mystical double talk? How can someone who lived two thousand years ago be in me as my contemporary? Let me explain. First of all, the English term "Christ" comes to us from the Greek *Christos*, which is translated from the Hebrew *Messiah*. *Messiah*, for the Hebrews, meant "the anointed one," one who serves a high mission, fulfills a holy office, or is involved in a sacred mission. "Messiahs" have been kings, high priests, patriarchs. Christ is the expression of the highest purpose of God to which Jesus gives a human face. Christ is Jesus, but Christ as an office is our calling too. Therefore, when Paul spoke of Christ within, he is identifying himself with the spirit that made Jesus what he was, that being the Christ.

All this may seem very esoteric and difficult to understand, but when you're talking about a new person, the Christ, the spirit of Jesus living in you, growing in you, this is a subject that stretches language to the breaking point. Paul put it as best he could: "To whom God would make known what is the riches of the glory of this mystery among the Gentiles; which is Christ in you, the hope of glory..." (Col. 1:27, KJV).

As the relationship of human-divine interaction continues, the Kingdom of God is given an opportunity for expression—that is, you begin to see it proceeding from your life into the larger human scene even in times of crisis large and small. When in former times there would have been nothing but corners of crisis, now there are spaces of tranquility and joy. Where there has been the crisis of failure, victories are reported; where there has been the crisis of despair, now there is reason to hope. Where there has been the crisis of discord, now there are moments of harmony. Where there has been the crisis of fear, it is gradually replaced by faith. Truth begins to make inroads against falsehood. Even the crisis of death is no longer so ultimate a dread. However, none of this is self-evident, nor from an outward point of view is it natural. Because the strategy in crisis is not ours, it is of God. So it is with things of the Spirit.

It's like Paul speaking of the Kingdom of God being in you and then saying that you are in the Kingdom of God. The idea that God is in you but at the same time you are in God; that Christ is in you and that you are in Christ; that you are a temple of God and that God is in that temple—all seems ambiguous. If you're troubled by these paradoxical expressions having to do with contingencies of time and space, then just be aware that this is a problem of the inadequacy of the outer order language trying to speak on behalf of the inner. In times of crisis, it makes no difference whether we live in Christ or Christ lives in us. What is important, as Paul put it, is this: "For me to live is Christ..." (Phil. 1:21). What he's saying is that we are no longer living totally in the physical realm. When trouble knocks at our door, a new tenant answers—and no trouble is so large as to intimidate the inner dweller. This is the spirit that was in Jesus, the living Christ in us—the Kingdom dweller.

So the next time you come to a crisis experience, realize that creative energy generated from God's transcendent Kingdom is available to you. However, in order to tap this resource, you must turn without hesitation to the summerland of God's grace, which requires a new self-estimate and knowledge based on Kingdom enlightenment.

One of the greatest manuscript finds since the discovery of the Dead Sea Scrolls was the 1945 unearthing of a clay jar near Nag-Hammadi in upper Egypt, which contained forty-eight Coptic gnostic works on some seven hundred pages that had been produced in Greek in about A.D. 140. One of the "Sayings of Jesus" from this collection feels so right that I must use it to close this chapter on the strategy of the Kingdom. Jesus is speaking:

> If those who lead you say to you: "see, the Kingdom is in heaven," then the birds of the heaven will precede you. If they say to you: "It is in the sea, then the fish precede you. But the Kingdom is within you and is without you. If you (will) *know* yourselves, then you will be *known* and you will *know* that you are the sons of the Living Father. But if you do not *know* yourselves, then you are in poverty and you are poverty."[3]

Notes

1. Edmund F. Perry, from the sermon "Where Does the Christian Religion Get Us After All?" Delivered at First United Methodist Church, Evanston, Illinois, August 5, 1979.
2. William Lecky, *History of European Morals* (D. Appleton and Company, 1898), vol. 1, p. 424.
3. A. Guillaumont, ed. and trans., *The Gospel According to Thomas* (New York: Harper & Brothers, 1949), p. 3.

CHAPTER 4

The Pathway of Love's Lessons

IN TIMES of crisis, many turn to God for comfort. Christians are familiar with the gracious words of Jesus, "Come unto me, all ye that labor and are heavy laden, and I will give you rest." However, the picture of Jesus as consoler, comforter, and healer—accurate as it is—is still incomplete.

There is little doubt that Jesus was, among other things, a demanding teacher. He did not teach abstract metaphysics or a catechism-like system of theology. He taught through his daily experience with lessons that his followers needed to learn before others could be given. The problem, both ancient and contemporary, is that many keep going from the same problem to the same problem, from the same crisis to the same crisis, without learning the lessons that are implicit; the only difference being new names, faces, and settings.

It is difficult to think of Jesus as a demanding teacher. It is much easier to be enamored of the sweet, sentimentalized picture of our Lord that we have from childhood. He was and is in spirit a beautifully loving presence. But unfortunately his love is misunderstood as passive acceptance. We have been taught through the doctrine of atonement that Jesus poured out his love for us on the cross at Golgotha. There, we are told by the theologians, he paid the penalty for our sin incurred by Adam in the primordial Fall. He offered himself as sacrifice before the offended justice of God. In fact, according to many theologians, this is Christ's function in the cosmos: forever interceding on our behalf before the throne of God. Such an unfathomable service of love apparently can only be accepted.

According to this teaching, Jesus' sacrificial death was intended to produce such horror and shock among those for whom he died that it would somehow permanently affect the spirit of humanity. This offering of himself was intended to kindle in the hearts of all people a love for Jesus because of what he did for them. If we've been taught any Christian theology at all, we have been made aware of the huge price that was paid for our salvation. The death of Jesus convicts us of our sins and our inherited bent to sinning.

I am unspeakably grateful for what Jesus did, but the question still remains: "What lessons have I learned from his sacrificial act, for myself and others?" Getting bailed out of a cosmic jail; being forgiven because of something someone has done for me; even the sacrifice of my Lord on the cross is not teaching me anything except that I am forever a spoiled, guilt-ridden child who has technically gotten off from punishment through the suffering of another. I know I'm supposed to regard this as a part of Christ's work for the human family, but I cannot help feeling that I have some role to play.

The chasm between God and the contemporary person is still enormous, despite what Jesus did on the cross. Though we say we love God because he first loved us and that his vicarious suffering saved us, we can't help but wonder if Christ's transaction for us has really made it right between God and ourselves. There is no time when all this questioning is more pronounced than in times of personal crisis.

To set the record straight, I believe that Christ's love is the most powerful force for good in all the world. It was Christ's love that drew out of the impulsive Simon the new man Peter. It was Christ's love that transformed an adulterous woman into a radiant saint. It was Christ's love that changed a self-despising tax collector into a man with self-esteem. It was Christ's love that reached out to the downtrodden of his society—particularly to women and children—and gave them a new sense of worth. It was Christ's love that worked miraculously on the lame, the halt, and the blind. It was Christ's love that appeared to have been repulsed by the conniving politicians of Jerusalem. It was Christ's love that was apparently humiliated in Pilate's judgment hall and subsequently defeated on the cross. But, in the end, it was Christ's love that proved conclusively that no sulking grave could contain his life-giving resurrection power.

The fact in faith is that each of us is a recipient of Christ's love, not just a beneficiary of a two thousand year old transaction. I believe that God's strategy is that we should be participants in the redemptive process and this active participation has a definite bearing on our response in times of crisis.

St. Paul has a few instructive words in this matter of sharing the life of Christ in the ultimate sense even to pain and death. He proclaimed, "I die daily" (1 Cor.

15:31); and, "I rejoice in my sufferings for your sake, and in my flesh I complete what is lacking in Christ's afflictions..." (Col. 1:24). Paul was so interpenetrated with Christ that he gave himself for others as Jesus did. He realized that a life shared with Jesus means co-dying as well as co-living. In other words, we have a responsibility in our own redemption. I am not promoting the error of good works in place of faith—rather, I'm enlarging on our capacity in Christ to allow him to reproduce his life and love through us, which is the life of Christ deed through Christ faith.

Jesus' death on the cross was indeed a vicarious one, but it was more. He was dying for us but he was also inviting us to participate on a new level of experience. This invitation to learn lessons from the great teacher must not be missed. In fact, Jesus was ever the teacher, even in his death. He taught that even you and I can share his death in our crisis times that, despite the circumstances, can lead to one personal resurrection after another. If you examine the cross experience, you will see that Jesus was not just suffering in our place, he was also suffering on our behalf—which gives a different slant to this event. Jesus invites us to share his life so that he can share ours. In fact, his strategy seems to be his willingness to penetrate our lives, even in times of crisis. He would be crucified through us in our various crises and resurrected through us in our triumphs day-by-day.

A man came to church one Sunday after having been tortured for three-and-a-half hours two nights previous. Robbers had broken into his house and, after collecting all the valuables they could lay hands on, proceeded to slash his body with a knife mercilessly. While the wounds were not deep they were many, and required innumerable stitches to close. If that was not enough, one of the thieves forced the nurse who was caring for his invalid wife into his car, drove her to a nearby park, and raped her. The wounded man came to worship that Sunday and looked up at the cross hanging above the altar in our sanctuary no longer as a spectator but now as a participant, having shared his personal crisis with Christ.

Jesus takes the events of our lives, even the negative ones, including crisis times, and teaches us to die to the gross outer factors that are often the very cause of our crises, that we may be born into a new life of participation in the resurrection drama. Whatever your problem, the underlying lesson to be learned may be that something in you must be crucified so that Christ can live fully through you; therefore, as you voluntarily take up your own cross you're on the way to overcoming through the power of Christ.

Transformation from the old person to the new is the central teaching of the gospel. It requires death to the old so the new life can emerge. It is an inner process of growth, especially in crisis times, from the old lower to the new higher level. Jesus insists that we put an end to the routine of self-justification and rationalization for not dying to the old self. The lessons of Christ have nothing to do with an increase of religious knowledge or how to cope with the world. Rather, they declare that you must crucify the old and become a new person.

You may be offended at my insisting that we all need to move up to a higher level of experience. We tend to become very self-righteous and self-satisfied where we are, particularly when threatened with perfection. We feel we must protect that to which we've become accustomed. Who in love dares to call you to the best you can be? We might even deride those who, choosing a new course of life, begin the crucifixion of the old for the sake of perfected new. We may accuse them of making the gospel too harsh. However, the demand-side of Jesus' love requires an all-out denying of the outer self, identification in spirit with Jesus' suffering on the cross. It renounces the old ways of self-promotion and urges the new way of self-surrender to follow the leading of Christ. At the center of this life is the mysterious process of death to life, as revealed in nature, where a grain of wheat must die as such in order to live as a new plant and bear new grains of wheat.

Too often Christian theology drags us back twenty centuries to confirm itself. If the cross is only viewed historically and read through the eyes of the ancient theologians, it ends up looking like a sacred legend at times more surrealistic than real. The fact is that what has won the devotion of the millions to Christ is his loving aliveness living through them. When Christ comes to live in a person, his life is reproduced in them. Crisis times may direct us to a cross where we might die externally to the old that we may live internally to the new. Even in the crisis that seems unto death, we are still being energized by his triumphant spirit. Negative crisis can never defeat us when the love of Christ is living in and through us. The message of St. Paul was that Christ can be alive in each person. God's love in Christ in us is the living testimony that won the ancient world.

Auguste Sabatier once wrote:

> Merely to repeat His words is not to continue His work; we must reproduce His life, passion and death. He desires to live again in each one of His disciples in order that he may continue to suffer, to bestow himself, and to labor in and through them towards the redemption of humanity, until all prodigal and lost children be found and brought back to their Father's house. Thus it is that, instead of being removed

far from human history, the life and death of Christ once more take their place in history, setting forth the law that governs it, and, by ceaselessly increasing the power of redemptive sacrifice, transform and govern it, and direct it towards its divine end.[1]

Jesus as the teacher of sharp-edged love taught always from a Kingdom point of view, even in times of crisis; in fact, he was known to precipitate a crisis to bring about a new teaching. It might be interesting to note some of these crisis lessons in various recorded situations. For example, he strategically shook the foundations of those who were living from an outer orientation—not the least of which were his own disciples—even though on the surface they appeared religious. I am convinced that he was not very much impressed with outward manifestations of spiritual power—that is, the demonstration of the so-called supernatural phenomena that produce tingling sensations, fascinations, and marvels. He knew that you can experience all these manifestations and still be lacking in wisdom and enlightenment.

I have heard that it is possible to have a vision or some lofty spiritual experience purely on the basis of physiological or psychological conditioning. For instance, if you should cut yourself off from sensory input—go on retreat, get away into absolute silence, or stare at an object for a long period of time, focusing your vision on that and that alone—you may, after a time, see something that looks like a spiritual being. But the question remains, what have you learned from the experience?

A Jesuit professor once explained that when nurses leave a hospital after working a double shift, they go into a chapel, kneel down at the altar, and see the face of Jesus. Actually, what they may be experiencing is an imbalance in the blood level—from sleep deprivation. Very often, because of inadequate oxygen intake to the brain, people see Jesus or an angel or their mother and father at the time when they are dying. Turn up the oxygen—and the vision vanishes. So what have they learned?

It is reported that seventy of Jesus' followers returned from an evangelistic mission excited about how even the demons had been subject to them. They were caught up in the ecstasy of spiritual happening. He countered them with, "Do not rejoice in this, that the spirits are subject to you; but rejoice that your names are written in heaven" (Luke 10:20). In other words, outer demonstrations, including spiritual highs, psychic fireworks, and mechanically induced fantasies, are insignificant compared to the inner teaching relationship that is the source of all power.

John the Baptist could not understand this approach. In fact, it plunged him into a crisis of doubt, wondering if Jesus was really the Messiah—"the one who was to come." He wanted Jesus to use his superhuman powers to overcome the external forces of evil that he identified with the Roman military occupation of his country. He desired that Jesus demonstrate outward signs and wonders to establish a new revolutionary government. But Jesus was not interested in being a wonder-working political Messiah. Jesus the master teacher could certainly understand the motivation of John. He regarded the Baptist as the greatest man born of woman. But, as he put it, "Yet he who is least in the Kingdom of God is greater than he" (Matt. 11:11). It is not that great works are to be discouraged—healings, transformations, revelations, and the whole gamut of miraculous phenomena have their place, but only if they are the by-products of a lesson learned. This is the strategy of God for crisis times and other times as well.

When I was a child, I used to sit between my mother and father in Sunday worship services. I can still remember how hard the pews were. My father would give me a pencil so that I could draw pictures on the back of the bulletin and special collection envelopes. Growing tired of that, I would gaze at the stained glass window where Jesus was surrounded by children and lambs, all looking so stylized and content. He seemed predictably friendly and loving but I must say, most of all, he seemed pathetically boring.

It took me a long time to realize that this is not the living word of Jesus presented in the New Testament, and anyone who thinks it is hasn't read the Scripture. He was, of course, a lover of children and, I suppose, animals too. But he is and was a demanding teacher who teaches with the sword of the spirit and often used a crisis experience as a metaphor for explanation and emphasis. This is not to say that he purposely caused or causes people hardship in order to teach them a lesson. I've heard every kind of human tragedy, catastrophe, and accident attributed to being "God's will," which gives rise to a basic confusion about the nature of God and the world in which we live. We have this ridiculous idea that somehow God is always on the side of winners, whether in war, business, football games, or affairs of the heart. All of this is based on an outward view of life.

Jesus taught that we need to change our minds and start living from another perspective. For instance, in the Lord's Prayer, Jesus taught us to pray—"Thy Kingdom come, Thy will be done on earth as it is in heaven" (Matt. 6:10). In this prayer, Jesus is saying that the will of God is not done on earth unless we embody that will. His Kingdom is not on this level unless we incarnate it. All the pain, misery, and unhappiness connected with life in this world is not a part of God's will. Rather, it is a product of life fixed on the lower level that perishes and dies without meaning. However, all the crises of our outer lives can be the stuff through which the lessons of Christ come, not necessarily with answers easily found in the back of a theological lesson book, but by the help of God working through assorted crisis challenges. Usually, our problems reflect the earthbound situation. But, when earth is our only home, what else can we expect? On the other hand, when the physical is no longer the central focus of our lives and we have begun to realize our prior citizenship is in the Kingdom of God, then that which is lower can be transformed by that which is higher—which appears to be the strategy of Christ.

Christ's love is not always a comforting aura. It can be surgical, antiseptic, and purging. It can bring on a crisis fever to burn out the impurities of our lives. It never failed that when the disciples were beginning to feel overconfident in their relationship with Jesus, he instigated a crisis of spirit that sent them searching for spiritual resources he had planted in them. Jesus was always trying to free his disciples from an unhealthy dependence on himself. He wanted these people to grow in his light and not his shadow. Perhaps the reason his ministry lasted no longer than three years was that he found that the disciples were never going to make any real strides toward spiritual maturity as long as he was physically present.

On one occasion, as they were making their way through the countryside, the disciples were feeling particularly locked into him on the child-level of proprietary rights, as a child will say "This is *my* Daddy." Jesus suddenly stopped and began conversing with a little man perched on the branch of a sycamore tree. It happened that this man, Zacchaeus, was a tax collector; in fact, he was a chief tax collector. From Zacchaeus' point of view, being noticed by Jesus was an astonishing, once-in-a-lifetime experience. He was hated by nearly everyone from one end of the country to the other. Though he suffered from deep ridicule (tax collectors working for a foreign occupation government were despised as the scum of the earth), he had been unable to wean himself from his profitable work. More than its transforming effect on Zacchaeus, the exchange must have been a staggering blow to the egos of the disciples. As far as they were concerned, their Lord and master addressing such a person was an enormous embarrassment bordering on the scandalous. To make matters worse, Jesus even invited himself to be a guest at the home of Zacchaeus. For the tax collector, this was a dream come true. It was the high point of his entire existence. As for the disciples, it was a shocking incident, further aggravated by the conversation they overheard between Jesus and his host. Zacchaeus said to him, "Behold Lord, the half of my goods I give to the poor; and if I have defrauded anyone of anything I restore it fourfold" (Luke 19:8). Jesus' response left the disciples shaken: "Today salvation has come to this house, since he also is a son of Abraham. For the son of man came to seek and to save the lost" (Luke 19:9-10). Undoubtedly, the disciples were caught up in an emotional crisis; but it was the disturbance of immaturity. They had been living too long in a superficial relationship with Jesus, and he was correcting this error with a sharp-edged lesson. Jesus was, for his followers, the instrument of God's love taking the misunderstanding in relationship and transforming it into something profound and enduring.

Reading the gospel record in present tense as a series

of spiritual lessons makes Jesus, the teacher, painfully our contemporary. Remember when his disciples had been anxious that they might perish in a storm at sea? Jesus wounded them with a sharp indictment: "Why are you afraid, O men of little faith?" (Matt. 8:26). There was nothing Jesus emphasized more than "having faith," and to be accused of not having it would have been like getting an "F" on a term paper. Consider the incident when nine of his disciples failed to heal an epileptic boy. He tongue-lashed them with the most cruel words: "O faithless and perverse generation, how long am I to be with you?" (Matt. 17:17). In truth, this sort of "reading out" was not a rare happenstance between Jesus and his followers. But it was never done without love. Love can wound in the course of teaching, but it heals when truth is realized.

Observe the contrast in his teaching method on another occasion. He whirls his friends around with the most incredible praise: "You are [note the use of the straightforward present tense—not "maybe" or "hopefully"] the light of the world" (Matt. 5:14). To the same "faithless and perverse ones" he gives an astounding assignment: "You therefore must be perfect as your heavenly Father is perfect" (Matt. 5:48). This is what I mean by insisting that Jesus was and is a teacher with a variety of lessons, fermenting crises of spirit to apply the teaching of love. Jesus is a teacher who identifies our weaknesses, our mediocrities, our low-level obsessions. If we let him, he will remorselessly smash away at anything holding us captive to an outer form—that is, if we're willing to be taught.

Some have unwisely attempted to make a religion out of the harsh words of Jesus, not realizing (perhaps on purpose) that love always motivated his words. He could be reproachful, but he could also be so loving that to read his words is to be blessed by divine warmth. "Take my yoke upon you, and learn of me; for I am gentle and lowly in heart, and you will find rest for your souls. For my yoke is easy, and my burden is light" (Matt. 11:29-30). Jesus speaks to one person for one need and to another for an entirely different problem. But the strategies of love are always the same. It is to promote transformation from the lower to the higher life.

A fascinating aside in Jesus' teaching ministry was his relationship with women. If you had been a woman during his lifetime, you would not have enjoyed the same status as a man. "Woman's position in the Bible is largely that of subordination to her father or her husband. In several instances the word for 'wife' signifies woman belonging to man (Gen. 2:24-25; 3:8, 17; 4:1, 17)."

"Woman's inferior status however is reflected in laws that show discrimination: A daughter is less desirable than a son (Lev. 12:1-5); she could be sold for debt by her father (Exod. 21:7; cf. Neh. 5:5): she could not be freed at the end of 6 years, as could a man (Lev. 25:40). She could be made a prostitute by her father (Judg. 19:24). The man had the right of Divorce. The valuation of a man differs from that of a woman when a special vow is made (Lev. 27:1-7)."[2]

Women were always present in Jesus' ministry, and must have been among the crowds that he addressed. On one occasion, he was speaking to a large gathering on his favorite subject, the Kingdom of God. He began by saying that the Kingdom of Heaven is like yeast some women put in three measures of meal (Luke 13:20-21). For Jesus to connect the Kingdom of God with the commonplace action that a woman knew best—that of baking bread—was little less than a crisis blow to the minds of the Jewish men in his audience. But suddenly the women of the crowd had come alive. Jesus, unlike most of the other religious leaders, was talking to them about what they could relate to—putting some yeast in bread. He understood! It may have been a crisis in spirit for the men, but it was a loving affirmation of worth to the women. But for both there was a lesson to be learned. This was part of God's love strategy.

Another one of these crisis-producing teachings occurred at Jacob's well in Samaria, when Jesus lovingly conversed with a beleaguered Samaritan woman. It was to this Samaritan female (whose race the Jews considered a social anathema), whose religious attitudes were at best unorthodox, that he revealed not only his clearest definition of God but a revelation of his own identity as well. He even told her how to worship. The disciples must have again been flabbergasted, provoking a crisis in spirit. It is said that they "marveled." Probably they marveled not so much at what he said but to whom he said it. To think he would say all those glorious things to a woman, and a half-breed Samaritan at that.

In answer to her question as to where was the best place of worship—Mount Gerizim or in Jerusalem—Jesus followed no party line response when he said, "Woman, believe me, the hour is coming when neither on this mountain nor Jerusalem will you worship the Father.... But the hour is coming, and now is, when the true worshippers will worship the Father in spirit and in truth, for such the Father seeks to worship him. God is spirit, and those who worship him must worship in spirit and truth" (John 4:21-24). However upsetting the lesson, it was given out of love for the spiritual health of all the hearers.

The journey in spiritual growth is as well a pilgrimage

into trying to think God's thoughts by his spirit. As you remember, this was part of the rebuke Jesus made against Simon Peter when Jesus accused him of not being on the side of God (Matt. 16:23). Our sensate orientation of going with the crowd is often the cause of spiritual imbalance, because so much on the physical level is a distortion of truth. Our becoming aware of the real goal in life instigates frequent testings and spiritual crises along the way. For those seeking to live a transformed life, Jesus promised that he would send his spirit, that inner loving companion of truth to guide us into all truth.

Last summer, my wife and I were faced with a crisis that in former times would not have been a crisis at all. Three churches had sought me out almost at the same time, requesting that I become their senior minister. We were, of course, flattered by the phone calls, letters, and visits of committees from far away places. But something was wrong. The problem is that when you seek to live from the Kingdom level, the old ways of operating become obsolete. Our question was not so much *should* we move, but *why*. Always before we would probably have been interested in taking the next larger church up the so-called ladder of success, but now there were higher considerations. Still, the offers were attractive and the idea of a new challenge did have appeal. I remember one of my professors in graduate school making this unequivocal statement, "When the next, largest church calls you—you drop everything and go. This is what your career is all about—moving up."

The problem was that, as we attempted to be more surrendered to God, the idea of "moving up" was not our chief priority; in fact, as far as the Kingdom of God is concerned, it seemed irrelevent. The heart tugs came when well-meaning friends, learning of our offers, could not understand our lack of enthusiasm for getting ahead professionally. They didn't seem to realize that for us the old operating procedures were no longer in force.

Then my wife, Natalie, found a little twelve-foot styrofoam sailboat on sale, and she ordered it with great excitement. As soon as the boat arrived, we went to claim it, only to discover that there was a small nick in its hull. After some negotiation, we were given twenty dollars off the sale price. Arriving home with great anticipation, we removed the sail from its package. Lo and behold, it bore the name and the seal of a prominent beer company. I've never seen my wife so angry. She pronounced with all the indignation she could muster, "I refuse to sail under the colors of a beer company." Back to the store we marched for another round of negotiations. Once again, a kindly credit supervisor gave us still another discount. In all, the boat turned out to be practically a gift.

Later, after Natalie had manufactured her own sail, we were frequently out on our lake sailing to and fro reflecting, meditating, and praying about our vexing situation. Deadlines were now being made, the crisis was coming to a head. Our prayer was, "Lord, lead us as you will in your own time and in your own way." As the days wore on we became more relaxed about our situation, as if it really had been placed in God's hands. Then, one special afternoon as the sun was setting and we were being pushed along by a gentle wind—Natalie at one end of the boat and I at the other, our feet lightly touching—something happened that altered our lives. We were overtaken by the love of our Lord. That is, we became recipients of a strategy of his love even in that time of crisis.

I had closed my eyes and was listening inwardly, more focused than usual, when some words began to form in my consciousness. They were very clear, almost pedantic, and stabbed away at my consciousness; "Your whole life has been that of competition. Always you have been trying to get ahead and advance yourself professionally. It is time to behold a new way. I will give you the gift of contemplation. Open your eyes." I opened my eyes and the first object in my line of vision was, of course, my wife's face. Everything in me came to a halt. I stared at her in astonishment. Her face glowed with a radiance that I can only describe as angelic. She seemed to reflect a prism of rays across the water and into the sky. Those beams of light gave everything they touched an ethereal quality that softly pulsated and sparkled. Turning my head I was dazed by the sunset—the colors so incredible that several months later I can still remember them. The lake, clear enough to see the bottom, became a washed glass pool of enchantment inviting observation into a whole new world waiting to be discovered.

The dimensions of nature seemed to have converged like a group of gifted musicians who gather for a jam session that grows into a concert. I wished that it would last an eternity, which was exactly what was happening. Later, I realized that I had been involved in the eternal now. I have never felt such joy. Most of all, I was in love with where I was. I kept saying, "Thank you Father," as if there were nothing else to say.

Crisis time or not, you can reject what the world dictates. You can allow the Lord to take possession of your life by letting go of the old moorings and allowing his loving spirit to guide you. Let me remind you that this is a very subtle process. What's more, you can't take credit for the transformation going on within because the work is not yours. It is the strategy of God. Anyhow, how could you congratulate yourself for something that was given to you as a gift of love?

As a closing note, sometimes people operate as teaching instruments of the Lord quite without realizing it. Who knows, even an adversary may be working a love lesson on you right now that is part of the strategy of God. It could be the boss who has been giving you a hard time, the neighbor who is a trial, the frustrating friend. The comic-tragic human drama in your business, or any of your human relationships within a church, or a club that seems to be acting against you, but for a purpose. Taking an aspirin or a Valium, getting drunk, flying off to someplace for a change of scenery is not a solution to anything. You need to examine the problem from the point of view of a spiritual teaching.

A few years ago, scientist-poet Loren Eiseley wrote something that has stuck in my mind and lends itself to what I am trying to express now. He told about getting up early one morning, heading down to the beach and observing off in the distance a man reaching down and lifting up drifting starfish that had made their way from the ocean depths to the shoreline in an effort to dig into the safety and security of the deep wet sand, thus putting an end to their evolutionary struggle for life. Again and again he hurled them as far out as he could on the rolling sea, forcing them to swim once more; for to remain beached would result in certain death. Eiseley called him the "star thrower."[3]

At this point in my life's journey, when I reflect on the crisis-like sandy places in which I've been stuck—not the least of which was my "bland predictable" Jesus image—I recall, now with great appreciation, those loving, star-throwing, Jesus-like teachers who extricated me from the wet sand, flinging me out to the wider sea of new adventure. Come to think of it, I can scarcely remember who they all were—but it makes no difference because they were in fact God's forces, God's loving energy patterns, alternately friend and foe—all agents of God's strategy of love for my life.

Christian theologians have long focused on Jesus' revealing God to us, and have neglected how gloriously he revealed us to ourselves. I contend that in crisis time, like any other time, we have a special opportunity by the love teachings of God to "grow in wisdom and understanding."

Teilhard de Chardin puts it very well:

> So let us bow our heads in tribute to the anxieties and joys of "trying all and discovering all." The passing wave that we can feel was not formed in ourselves. It comes to us from far away; it set out at the same time as the light from the first stars. It reaches us after creating everything on the way. The spirit of research and conquest is the permanent soul of evolution.[4]

Notes

1. August Sabatier, "The Atonement," from Rufus M. Jones, *The Double Search* (Philadelphia: Winston, 1937), p. 56.
2. Otto J. Babb, in *The Interpreter's Dictionary of the Bible* (Nashville: Abingdon, 1962), vol. 4, pp. 865, 866.
3. Loren Eiseley, *The Unexpected Universe* (New York: Harcourt Brace Jovanovich, 1969), pp. 67–92.
4. Jeanne Mortier and Marie-Louise Aboux, eds., *Teilhard de Chardin Album* (New York: Harper & Row, 1966), p. 133.

CHAPTER 5

The Pathway of Prayer

CRISIS MAKES pray-ers of us all. Though we may know very little about prayer, most of us have a certain reverence for it. Prayer for most is closing our eyes, bowing our heads, clasping our hands, and trying to say a few appropriate words to God. Perhaps what we need is a specific guideline on how to pray effectively in times of crisis rather than a discussion on the general philosophy of prayer.

We read in the Old Testament that God instructed Noah to build an ark following an unusual and provocative design. Beside a closed door, it had only one other opening, a window that faced up. God ordered Noah, "A window shalt thou make to the ark and in a cubit shalt thou finish it above" (Gen. 6:16, KJV). I have no reason to believe that this design was accidental. Imagine what would have happened if the ark had been equipped with no other opening except several port holes on a horizontal line along the hull of the ship. The human occupants would probably have huddled around the nearest porthole looking out on the horizon, anxiously speculating as to whether or not God was still in charge. With each nervous observation from their limited perspective, Noah's crew would have had increasing reason to grumble about the horizontal problems: "The water is still rising." "When will the rain ever stop?" "No land in sight anywhere—has God forsaken us?" "No birds to be seen, just water and more water. When will this ever end?" "There's nothing out there—God doesn't care!" Whether it be ancient or contemporary, the perspective at this level is always the same. It sees nothing but the severity of the storm, the darkness of the clouds, how long the bad weather has lasted or will last, and—of course—the absence of God.

The foregoing script needs no updating. It's as timely as what we may have been thinking while watching the TV news this morning. The present crisis of energy shortages, inflation, hunger, threats of war, plus our personal problems are like the gathering of dark clouds threatening ominous storms. The question is, how do we prepare ourselves to meet these crises? The answer is as specific now as it was in the days of Noah, when God commanded that an ark be built following a specific design that included a window facing up. I think we are under the same kind of orders, only this time the arks are our personal lives and constructing the opening upward is a matter of getting serious about the discipline of prayer.

A dear old friend once told me to pray by periodically aligning myself with God. At the time, I wasn't sure what he meant; but lingering in the midst of a crisis or two, I was willing to try anything. The idea is to try and line up your thoughts with the will of God, as you understand it, about every fifteen minutes of your waking hours. It is a formidable discipline in concentration. What astonished me most in trying to get into this alignment was the importance of little things. I was dismayed how often I felt out of God's will because of some insignificant word or deed, a look, an attitude, a passing thought. Perhaps one of the reasons that we do not achieve our full spiritual potential is that we are undermined by negative trivia. We may be missing the Kingdom for lack of concentration. The disciplines of trying to align our will with that of God every fifteen minutes can be, if nothing else, a great learning experience in the way our minds operate ... but mostly, it is a strategy of God.

Recently, I attended a runners' clinic to hear a sports physician speak on the subject of alignment. Having worked with hundreds of athletes involved in a variety of sports activities, he has concluded that stress and poor performance result from improper alignment of the skeletal body. He stated unequivocally that if we are not in proper body alignment, our circulation is impaired and our organs are pushed out of place. The result is disease. He taught us how to stand in the proper posture, visualizing a plumb line stretching down from the forehead across the chest, across the stomach, across the pelvic bone, and falling between the feet. He taught us how to walk by striding and maintaining the proper posture.

On stage with him was one of our country's finest female runners. After the lecture I talked with her about her experience with alignment. She showed me the scars on her legs from surgery that she said would have been unnecessary if she had known about the principle of alignment. Furthermore, she declared that all of her recent record-breaking runs have come since she learned to line up her body properly.

While prayer is our most powerful method of connecting with God, it is only as good as our alignment in spirit. Checking our will with that of God is to the spirit what lining up in perfect posture is to the physical. Our spiritual forefathers, the Pilgrims, who came to this country seeking religious freedom, knew something about the principle of alignment. They believed in beginning each day with a prayer and a psalm so as to synchronize themselves with God. If you are truly serious about developing a prayer life that will prevail through all the seasons of life, including crisis times, then I urge you to start each day aligning yourself first with the Lord's Prayer, followed by the Twenty-third Psalm.

Let me suggest praying the Lord's Prayer in the following meditative fashion, which may prove a God-given strategy for your praying in crisis times.

Our Father
Fix your eyes on God as the all-loving, all-powerful, all-perfect Father and your relationship to him as that of his son or his daughter. Keep a steady gaze on him in all of his glory, joy, and peace. Now feel your petty disturbances, hates, selfish desires, little lusts, greeds, envies, slipping off like filthy rags. Bathe yourself in the purity of his presence. Be clean; be whole.

Which art in heaven
We know where heaven is. Jesus told us that it is within. It is at the invisible depth point. It is an inner dimension with which I can have contact right now. It can flow through my life. If I really desire heaven to be here and now, I must seek it with all my heart. Something in me clamors for that native home.

Hallowed be thy name
Ancient people believed that a person's name was synonymous with his or her power. Therefore to know a person's

name was to know the secret of his or her power. God's name is above our knowing because God and humankind are not on the same level. What is lower is not in contact with the higher. Thus we would lift to God a persistent openness, allowing the higher level power to work upon us.

Thy Kingdom come, thy will be done on earth as it is in heaven
This is the petition for transformation. We pray that the highest can be realized in our lives. This is a lifetime prayer requiring constant attention to the will of God. This is the highest prayer that we can pray in terms of the world in which we live, for we are literally praying that through us the Kingdom of God will be manifested and that his will will be done through us into the world.

Give us this day our daily bread
The need for physical food is important to maintain our physical well-being, but having spiritual food is even more important. Jesus was well aware of our physical needs; but, in this instance, he is praying for transsubstantial food or spiritual food that we need every day, just as we need the physical food.

Forgive us our debts as we forgive our debtors
Forgiveness is release. If we do not forgive, we bind and imprison ourselves to the lower level. Canceling grievances, hates, resentments is a way of gaining freedom from the external life. Releasing and letting go of all past negative feelings frees a person in a marvelous way.

Lead us not into temptation, but deliver us from evil
As you align yourself with God, you request that your outward, human reasoning not be in charge of your life through this day. The temptation to trust what is seen externally is great but in the long run, it produces the worst possible results.

For thine is the kingdom and the power and the glory forever
The sum total of all of our praying is seeking the Kingdom of

God filled with the power and glory of God. This is our highest goal of attainment. This is the true aim of prayer. All our praying should concentrate on this supreme purpose.

Next let us practice aligning ourselves on the Twenty-third Psalm.

The Lord is my shepherd
First of all, the Lord God Almighty is the shepherd of us all. As is true with shepherds in general, God calls each of his sheep by name. He knows our special needs. He offers us love and protection. Notice the personal relationship, "The Lord is my shepherd." God is my God.

I shall not want
If we walk with our shepherd and do not wander from the path, we are cared for in a wonderful way. It is reported that, in ancient times, when the sheep grew so old that they had lost their teeth, the shepherds would chew their grass for them, masticating it thoroughly and placing it in their mouths for them to swallow so that they would not be in need.

He makes me lie down in green pastures. He leads me beside still waters
It is a shepherd's duty to seek out the most abundant pastures for his sheep. This is why he pastures his sheep in different places at different times of the year. It is also true that because of the peculiar shape of the sheep's nose, they have difficulty drinking water, particularly running water. Therefore the shepherds will frequently dam up a stream, making the water relatively still so that the sheep can drink comfortably. God, the good shepherd, is the provider for his sheep, according to the Psalmist.

He restores my soul
This is an affirmation of knowing God is working in my life. All my problems come about when I am separated from that knowing. The knowledge that God is working in my life is

like the sound of a reed instrument that is played to soothe the sheep.

He leads me in the paths of righteousness for his name's sake
The Psalmist is not talking about external righteousness that can be maintained in the eyes of the world. Righteousness is a life that is being led from the Kingdom point of view. Jesus spoke of not letting the left hand know what the right hand is doing. The right hand path is a higher level of life. The left hand way is on the lower level. When we are living the will of God, we do our good, for the applause of no one except God.

Even though I walk through the valley of the shadow of death, I fear no evil; for thou art with me
The key word here is "through." The Psalmist, wise in the ways of God, knew that no matter how dark the valley, he would prevail. They would not remain in the valley of shadows, but would walk through and come out on the other side.

Thy rod and thy staff, they comfort me
The rod is a club used to beat off any predators that might attempt to harm the sheep. The staff is the long pole with a crook on one end that is used to punch into holes where snakes might be lurking. It is also used to ward off threatening animals. It might even save a sheep that has gotten hung up in some hazardous place. It is within the province of the shepherd to protect and care for the sheep.

Thou preparest a table before me in the presence of my enemies; thou anointest my head with oil, my cup overflows
When we are with God and we sense God's presence in our lives, whatever the crisis, we have an inner fellowship that is like being in the most honored banquet room. In ancient times, an ordinary banquet assumed the proportion of a feast when oil was poured over the head of the guest. Nothing is lacking on this spiritual banquet table. Even our cup can't be

emptied. This is a picture of our inner relationship to God despite whatever is happening in the outer world.

Surely goodness and mercy shall follow me all the days of my life; and I shall dwell in the house of the Lord for ever.
This means simply that I am a part of God's household. I am one of his family and the house in which I will live eternally is larger than any domain I can imagine. It is a house of heavenly mansions and there I will dwell forever and ever.

If this spiritual alignment strategy—that is, the use of the Lord's Prayer and the Twenty-third Psalm—is given priority status at the beginning of each day, you'll be amazed at how omnipresent God really is for you. You'll be able to get into prayer with greater excitement, joy, and indeed fulfillment than ever before. No one can do it for you. It is yours to discover. Nothing of this alignment method can be proven unless it is tried.

The most disciplined person I have ever known in the spiritual life was Frank Laubach, the famous literacy teacher. He was the one who instructed me to keep God in mind every fifteen minutes through the day. For him, this method led to extended periods of inner communion until he was at one with God through nearly all of his waking hours. Interestingly, he did not develop this way of praying until he had gone through a great personal crisis.

Dr. Laubach had been serving on the faculty of the Union Theological Seminary in Manila (the Philippines) when, much to his delight, he found himself being considered for the presidency of the seminary. There was nothing he desired more than this prestigious position. It was the highest goal of his life. He prayed earnestly that God would allow him to have this job, and he lobbied vigorously among his colleagues for their support. Alas, despite all his efforts, he was denied the presidency and in the aftermath he nearly dissolved in bitter disappointment. Feeling he had to get away from the seminary, he resigned his position and decided to do some missionary work on the island of Mindanao, in the Philippines. His challenge was the conversion of a tribe of fierce head hunters known as the Moros.

Choosing to work among these very difficult people was no doubt a self-imposed exile; in fact, a kind of martyrdom. He couldn't have chosen a more difficult task. It was as though he wanted to punish himself further by failing once again, and fail he did. He simply could not bridge the cultural-spiritual gap between himself and the Moros. He had some success in providing them with health services and education, but felt he was not sufficiently gaining their confidence to win them to Christianity. He was absolutely desolate, mired in a consuming personal crisis. At this point, he referred to himself as a "forty-six-year-old has been." Then began a daily prayer routine that took him to a lonely spot called Signal Hill.

It was here that he began his practice of keeping God in his consciousness throughout the hours of the day. The experiment had its problems because of the distracting thoughts that filled his mind. He was constantly dredging up remembrance of all his past failures. However, he found a way to deal with these besetting obstacles. He would speak his prayers aloud, which included confessions, petitions, and all kinds of feelings as an outpouring from his inner being. He also concentrated on the panorama of nature's moods. Sometimes he actually felt at one with the magnificent cloud formations or the glowing sunset or the continually changing weather. Eventually he discovered the true beauty of the place that he had been calling his "second prison of defeat." Even the water spouts on Lake Lanao took on the qualities of mystery, beauty, and wonder as focal points for his praying. It occurred to him that if "one could only forget himself entirely and enjoy the universe, how free one would be to get in tune with the Spirit." Later he saw all this as a process for his spiritual reconstruction—as he reflected "God was showing me His very heart—even the angels can do no more than that." This was God's strategy for Dr. Laubach.

Then it happened—a pivotal point in his life that transformed everything for him. He had climbed up to Signal Hill, his favorite retreat spot. He was pouring out to God a tearful confession of frustration and failure.

> As I stood on the top very much inclined to let the tears break out of my eyes, my tongue stopped talking to God and began talking from God to me: "Ah, little child, I have hurt you tonight, and now I feel sorry with you. All you have confessed is true, but I love you still. I love you for coming here and telling me about it. I love you for hungering after me. I love you for being willing to be better. That is all I ask of people. Ah, I have wanted to do so much for you as soon as you would allow it. Now, with a sore and lonesome heart you are ready. And after this torture I must pull you close to my heart, tiny little one."[1]

That experience occurred on February 10, 1931. Fifteen days later, he got his marching orders while lying on the warm earth of Signal Hill. God's message for Dr. Laubach was:

> When you are teaching the Moros to read, your art is to say as little as you can and leave them to say as much as they will. That is why I leave you to do and say as much as you can, while I say little. You learn by doing, even when you make mistakes and correct them. You are to be sons and

daughters of God, and now you are taking the first feeble steps of an infant. Every step you take alone is infinitely more important than you now imagine, because the thing I am preparing you for exceeds all you imagine. So the talking you do to me is essential. The talking others do to you, when they are trying to talk up to your expectations, is more important than the talks you give to them. This is the best way to act: Talk a great deal to me. Let others talk a great deal to you, appreciating everything fine they say and neglecting their mistakes.[2]

And with that, Frank Laubach was given the way to teach his literacy lessons—which eventually would become a heralded worldwide method by which millions of people would learn to read. Strangely enough, or perhaps not so strangely, the way was revealed in crisis time prayer. Dr. Laubach might have sought information on how to teach his literacy program from a million sources, gathering bits and pieces of mechanical data here and there. But I doubt if the lessons—more important, the strategies for the lessons—would have come to reality had it not been for those long periods or prayer in which God gave Frank Laubach his marching orders.

If Christian people would become aware of the tremendous spiritual power at their disposal, whether in or out of crisis, we would enter a new era in history. We give a name to each age representing the greatest power with which humans have been able to work. We have called this the space age. By the power of God, we might call the next world epoch the spiritual age.

The power of prayer is virtually an untapped resource. Jesus said to his friends,

> Truly, truly I say to you, he who believes in me will also do the works that I do; and greater works than these will he do, because I go to the Father. Whatever you ask in my name I

will do it, that the Father may be glorified in the son; if you ask anything in my name, I will do it. (John 14:12-14)

One thing that must be clearly understood is that the gifts of God through prayer do not belong to us. They are gifts of the spirit. The giving is totally God-given in the name and nature of Jesus Christ and to him belongs all the glory and the praise.

Now let us consider some other strategies for effective prayer, whether in or out of crisis. As we fasten more attention on God, beginning with our fifteen minutes of checking up on our alignment with God, we will find ourselves surrendering our wills more easily to the will of God. Then, when we pray, we do so much more selflessly. When self is too much involved in the process of praying, we block the channel of our receiving.

I believe that when God spoke to his creation in the Garden of Eden, saying, "Have dominion," he was issuing a command that has never been rescinded. Once, during a crisis time, I was telling a spiritual life teacher that I was having difficulty making a particular prayer connection. I asked him if he thought I was being blocked by the will of God or it was just a run of bad luck. "Nonsense!" he shouted, waving his fork while attacking a salad. "We are not just to sit back and accept the hand we've been dealt. The name of the game is persistence. Go back and read what Jesus taught about prayer. He told his disciples that "they ought always to pray and not lose heart" (Luke 18:1). Persistence is the key. Jesus did not say that prayer would produce easy answers simply because the higher level (God's level) and the lower level (our level) are so far apart. But constant persistence develops intensity, which hopefully becomes a point of purifying fire. Then our prayers can rise from the lower to the higher in a more refined condition.

THE PATHWAY OF PRAYER 87

The teacher insisted, "You must get definite about what you really want through thought, word, and action. You must realize that you are not on just one level; rather, you are involved with several levels of being at once, and each is in correspondence with the other." He explained, "We consist of a physical body and several spiritual bodies." Actually, "body" is an awkward way to speak of these varying dimensional vehicles. It is as difficult to express as it was for St. Paul to explain that he had been "caught up to the third heaven" (2 Cor. 12:2), about which he could not speak.

Think of these dimensional bodies as being like the layers of an onion. Let the outer dry skin represent the physical body; the next layer in would be the first heavenly body; the next, the second heavenly body; and so on until we reach the kernel at the center, which is the pure creative essence of God. Each of these several bodies occupies a separate plane of consciousness, yet each is connected with the others and all is in all. Each plane, in sequence from the outer physical shell, moving toward the center, is more subtle than the one before. From another observation point, the physical plane is the end product of an extended, behind-the-scenes inner plane activity that has been set in motion at the center or "kernel" of creation, producing what we see eventually as imperfectly manifested in the physical world. He further explained that the Jews believed that there were seven heavens, which explains the story about St. Paul being taken up into the third heaven.

The teacher further stated that you can exercise a direct effect on the physical plane by working on the inner planes—particularly the next one "in"—and learning to work with that first heaven plane produces observable results on the physical level. According to him, it is far better to exercise an influence on the inner plane than to be forever subservient to the "catch as catch can" responses we call our "lot" on the physical. In this sense, knowingly or unknowingly, we are moment-by-moment creating our own physical world through mastery or default. I had never heard this expressed anywhere... not in church, graduate school, or any professional places of religious teaching. Actually, I didn't even know that there were inner planes; in fact, I thought the teacher was a little crazy—but sometimes the heavenly strategy can boggle the outer mind.

There is no more effective first step in bringing something through from the first heavenly plane to the physical plane than by picturing whatever we desire in vivid, colorful terms. The teacher explained that, on the first heaven plane, everything works in the exact opposite to the way things work on the physical plane—that is, the finished product is there the moment that we conceive it. The challenge then is to bring the spiritual fact into physical materialization. Without question, a strong picturing technique is essential in serving this purpose. I want to post a warning here. We are not to move into these exercises of drawing our dreams into reality unless we are first aligned with the will of God. Just remember you might draw into your life a desired blessing that could very well turn out to be a curse. So make sure you are in strategic alignment with God before doing the work.

By its very nature the mind, according to my teacher, is a picturing instrument and is always at work visualizing something. Unfortunately, perhaps without realizing it, we are often picturing negatively, and these pictures will produce themselves in actuality. Many people, particularly in time of crisis, pray negatively because they are picturing this way, which just makes matters worse.

First we must learn to hold a desired picture in consciousness long enough that we become comfortable with it; or, to put it another way, that our subconscious accepts it. This may be facilitated by making a spiritual "treasure map" (as some metaphysical teachers call them) on which are placed large, colorful pictures clipped from magazines and newspapers of what you are visualizing in the heavenly planes—whether that be a way out of crisis, spiritual growth, health, love, friendship, job, financial help, world peace, whatever, and in the center you might place a picture of Jesus, and perhaps a scripture, such as, "Whatever you ask in prayer you will receive, if you have faith" (Matt. 21:22).

Above all, this work is to be kept secret. Next, write down on a piece of paper precisely what you want, but leave room for the spirit to give you what might better meet your needs. Speak your desire out loud, affirming and decreeing "in the name and nature of Jesus Christ I affirm and decree that this will come to pass." One should then follow through by writing or making the appropriate safety valve affirmation: that "the end result of this work should continue to flow for my ultimate good and the good of others until such time as it is no longer serving the will of God."

I wonder if Jesus was not using first heaven visualization when he fed five thousand people by the Sea of Galilee. Note the procedure he used as he first made an inventory of what was available on the physical plane and after discovering that he had only five loaves and two fishes, he "looked up to Heaven, and blessed and broke the loaves..." (Mark 6:41). Incidentally, the looking to Heaven appears to be an alignment procedure. There were other occasions when he did the same thing.

When he was faced with the crisis of raising Lazarus from the dead it is reported, "Then Jesus looked upwards and said, 'Father I thank thee that thou hast heard me'" (John 11:41). Jesus visualized via the love of God projected into the first heaven and saw the consummation of his desire for the people—that is, food for everyone. The next step was to visualize his desire coming into actual materialization. It goes without saying that Jesus had a well-exercised sphere of availability, which is essential in this sort of work. He knew that God always heard him. In this practiced knowing, he was able to focus his disciplined being into a highly magnified receiving instrument, becoming like a human cornucopia drawing the higher first heaven vibrations of food into materialization for the people.

Jesus not only believed and had faith . . . he was willing to exercise the power of visualization, which allowed him to engage the first heavenly plane in such a way that he could draw the already accomplished fact back through the magnifying instrument of his body into physical manifestation. He then proceeded to destroy the concept of limitation, that is, the mere five loaves and two fishes that had preoccupied the hungry people. He literally pulled apart the static images of that trifling amount of food and began sharing the broken pieces with the crowd, thus setting in motion a current of outpouring from the first heaven plane that may have elicited further sharing of stashed-away provisions by people in the crowd.

If visualization into a higher level is unacceptable to you in terms of praying, or thinking of another level or dimension is too great a stretch for your spiritual imagination, then let me refer you to one of our country's outstanding scientists. Dr. William G. Pollard, former chairman of the board at Oak Ridge Consortium of Universities, speaks of how he and other scientists have been

> impelled toward the concept that the observable universe of space and time must be immersed in some vastly greater, totally mysterious matrix or medium which may be called "SUPERSPACE." In the known universe we recognize four dimensions—length, depth, width, and time.... But "SUPERSPACE" conceivably could have as many as TEN DIMENSIONS.[1]

Recently, I found two definitions of prayer that may be helpful to you particularly in crisis times. Robert Collier maintains that in the Old Testament, the Hebrew words of prayer have a variety of applications. One he calls to our attention is the Hebrew term *Palal* (to pray), which he translates as, "To judge yourself to be a marvel of creation; to recognize amazing wonders deep within your soul." The other is from the spiritual life teacher, Thomas Kelly, who wrote, "Deep within us all there is an amazing sanctuary of the soul, a holy place, a Divine Center, a speaking voice to which we may continuously return." He identified the source of this voice as "the Shekinah of the soul," "The presence in the midst," "Christ—he is within us all."[4]

The idea of a speaking voice is fascinating. Years ago I asked a knowledgeable prayer teacher, who in many ways was a genius in the practical application of spiritual life, about the speaking voice of which Thomas Kelly had written. He said, "I know exactly what he's describing. You must not take your inner voice lightly, no matter how infrequent the communication. This is your God-self talking to you and you must learn to trust whatever subjective impressions come and act upon them. This will strengthen the confidence bridge between the outer and the inner person. You should take time out of each day and tune in. This is exactly what Jesus did and you should do the same."

So for the next two years he gave me exercises to perform that would help me "listen in." Aside from learning to relax my body from head to toe, which included a number of exercises that had to do with isolating body parts, letting them go limp, and observing the process with detachment, I learned to breathe deeply and fully. He did not insist that I do complicated breathing techniques—just simple exercises on expanding the lungs fully, and breathing in rhythmic cycles. These exercises were conducted while I was flat on my back keeping my spinal column straight (aligning it), relaxing, breathing deeply and in good rhythm. This whole procedure is similar in one sense to the stretching exercises athletes do before running. Being relaxed, pliable, and flexible is the key to greater endurance and less injury.

Next, I would concentrate on what my teacher called "the screen of the mind," asking God to give me pictures or impressions of that which I should be aware. After a few months, symbols of various kinds did begin to take shape on this inner screen, but the test was always interpreting what the symbols meant. This required a deeper communications contact.

Many times in those early sessions I'd see a few geometric shapes and would pick up some words accompanying them. I trusted that the words were supplied to interpret the symbols. But, mostly, both the symbols and the words had to do with obscure things of little consequence. Now and then something would come completely out of the blue, such as an intuitive hunch concerning something about to happen to another person. Then my teacher would say: "You must test the spirit, which is the same as testing your inner self! Go to the person about whom you've received the impression and ask for a confirmation on what you've picked up. If the person gets serious and asks you how you knew, then you can make a joke out of it and shift attention from yourself. The important thing is to test those impressions. Get comfortable about following up on them. This will lead to more significant experiences.[11]

For a long time I made it a habit to check out my impressions as soon as possible following reception. If I was with a friend and got an inner picture or voice communication about something having to do with him, I would either tell the person directly or write it down. Frankly, my impressions were often incorrect; but as time went on, I discovered it wasn't the impression that was wrong, it was my inability to read the flow of information. My advice to anyone is to continue testing, experimenting, and working with the inner guidance system no matter how clumsy your first efforts. The more it is practiced, the more vivid and helpful it will become and less subject to error. Believe me, nothing can be more beneficial to yourself or others in time of crisis than this kind of inner direction. Also, you will find it easier to get help for others and yourself.

I insist that anyone can do this! There is nothing at all mysterious about it. We all have the inner equipment to be in touch with the Living Presence channeled through as a ceaseless flow of data. Listening in is a disciplined art and learning to trust what you hear is a lesson in faith and a step up in spiritual growth. I repeat, the more you listen and act upon the listening, the better the quality of the transmission. As time goes on, you won't need to be in the position of having to inform another of some very trivial information—such as the title of the book she was reading last night—in order to confirm or prove something to yourself. As the inner becomes a more familiar and proven quantity, the information deepens. Utilitarian things, bread-and-butter issues, crisis events are still processed, but the current deepens. Your prayer life becomes less a seeking for something and more a time of abiding—being at one with the Father. In fact, even hours of crisis, when our need is so great, the greater sufficiency is just having the companionship of the Father who is always there.

Several times a week I go into deep listening with a concern, either my own or someone else's. After moving past the distracting clamors of the outer mind, the inner is heard like a still small voice—usually in total and distinct opposition to that about which the outer has been fussing. You learn to adjust to that. The inner presence is often countering what your outer person thinks is important. I must warn you this is the nature of the "inner-outer" relationship.

Recently, I was worrying about a financial situation that I had long ago checked out with the inner presence, who at the time assured me that everything was okay for my continued involvement; but, due to some negative developments, I was panicking on the surface about the prospects of the venture. Bothered by doubts that left me tossing and turning at night, I tuned again to the "inner" and was impressed with the same unruffled appraisal of the situation. I can still hear my "inner" voice, "Don't worry, everything is working out; just relax. I have given you the information that should be sufficient." Finally, I had to make up my mind which master I would serve—the inner or the outer. Fortunately, for the long term, I chose the inner and I thank God for his leading in prayer.

Occasionally, when I'm angry, my outer response will be typically aggressive. But if I give it half a chance the "inner presence" comes through pleading, "Forgive, you must forgive, if you do not forgive, you cannot be released, so let it go—give this entire matter to the Father. Peace, let there be peace, let everything flow in perfect love." I urge you to try this listening-in method of praying. If nothing else, it teaches you that prayer is truly a dialogue—part of which you may have been missing.

We must come to understand that, when we pray, we simply launch out on the strategy proven by Jesus. "Whatever you ask in my name, I will do it, that the Father may be glorified in the Son" (John 14:13). We are not trying to remind God of his promises or coax him to fulfill his responsibilities to us. For example, when we pray for another person in some crisis situations we should pray that the person for whom we're praying will be open to listening to the will of God. We are not telling anyone, including God, what to do; instead we are praying in the name and nature of Jesus Christ for others to receive the will of God into their lives and turn their minds toward his guidance.

Most people at one time or another have had the experience of either sending or receiving a telepathic message. We have discovered that distance is a relative factor in this kind of communication. The important considerations are the concentrated effort of the transmitter, the focus of the message, and the sensitivity of the hearer. Given the potential for high level communication, why can't we pray more effectively in crisis situations around the globe?

I am convinced that the prayers of many people across the world have saved us again and again from a full-scale war and eventual nuclear catastrophe. This I believe is part of the strategy of God for saving our world. Some of these praying people have been practicing what might be called directed prayer, which is a prayer method that follows closely the principle of thought transference, but by the power of the Holy Spirit goes deeper and more powerfully than any superficial telepathic effect.

You may be wondering how it is possible to transmit a directed prayer to someone who may be many miles away, who might be asleep the moment you are praying for him or her. Actually, this is the best time to send directed prayers to another person. While it is true that the conscious mind does sleep, it is equally true that the subconscious mind never sleeps, and it is the subconscious mind that houses the great life-changing potential. However, the subconscious mind is subject to the conscious mind. The conscious mind, with its powerful censor and various mechanisms of defense, can reject both harmful and good ideas that might be transmitted. In order to reach another person's subconscious mind at a time when reception is at its best, the time to pray is after that person has gone to sleep, when redemptive ideas can be introduced to the subconscious mind.

This theory rests on practiced, reliable case studies. Educators tell us that one of the finest ways to teach children the multiplication tables, the spelling of difficult words, or the working of abstract problems is to wait until the child is asleep; then sitting by the bedside, repeat over and over again the facts that need to be absorbed by the subconscious mind. Soon the child will discover much to his or her delight that the problem is mastered. (It is never wise to acquaint children with what you are doing in this regard; it would be cruel to rob them of their sense of accomplishment.) The playing of tape recordings while a person sleeps has also become a proven method of teaching.

In order to practice directed prayer to the subconscious

mind of another person, one must follow a few simple rules. (1) Begin by speaking the person's name, as clearly as possible, three times in succession, in order that the subconscious mind will be aroused and open to your suggestion; (2) it is best to broadcast to the subject soon after he or she has gone to sleep so that the subconscious mind will have the entire night to dwell on the idea communicated. People in prayer groups may often broadcast to someone throughout the night, but they should make sure that individually their messages are identical; and (3) keep the message simple but affirmative. A statement of God-centered intent may be as sharp as a sword. Above all, align your will to God's as you understand it, checking out the need and direction of your prayer transmission. Remain directed by the spirit of God through the entire process. Never let the exigencies of a crisis time tempt you to force your own will in a given situation.

Occasionally, I have the opportunity of speaking to people in retirement homes. There I find men and women with great spiritual capacity who are just marking time until they die. This is a tragic waste of spiritual resource. One evening I was speaking to a sizeable crowd at a retirement center. I informed the people of some of the pressing needs of the world and urged them to stop thinking of themselves and get on with the unfinished work that God is calling them to through directed prayer. I challenged them to establish prayer groups in their homes. After the talk, I was overwhelmed by the enthusiasm of those people. They were just waiting for such an idea. One lady rushed up with a smile on her face and exclaimed, "I've been waiting to hear a call like this for years, now I know what I can do. I'm ninety-three years old and still able to serve the Lord."

Teenagers, with their boundless energy, are another

untapped source of spiritual energy. If they can be taught early in life how to pray, consider how powerfully God will use their lives through the years. We should never hesitate to bring young people onto the battleground of our spiritual crisis. Let them take their rightful places as responsible people of God. Too long we have denied young people the opportunity of participating in spiritual challenges because we were afraid that either they might not be interested or they might fail and we wanted to protect them.

If you agree with the validity of an inner-directed prayer effort, would it not seem a wise course of action to initiate a great inner-directed prayer offensive? All of us who believe in prayer should regularly transmit messages across the world to the Kremlin, to Iran, to Afghanistan, to all of the places where we sense the entrenchment of evil. Furthermore, we should pray using all the visual aids at our disposal. We should use maps to spot strategic target locations for our praying, and other information including the name of people and institutions, including pictures of people and places to help make more effective our visualizations for prayer. However, none of these artificial props should ever become so indispensable that we find ourselves unable to pray without the extra paraphernalia. We must remain flexible and free to move with the promptings of the Spirit.

Churches across America with already established prayer groups could develop an inner-directed prayer offensive without involving any other additional organization. Individual Christians who believe in this approach ought to begin at once; and if they find a few like-minded souls who share a common belief in this method of prayer, perhaps an inner-directed prayer group could be organized immediately. I believe that our praying ought to be specific and sharp-edged. That is, we should heed the inner voice and act. We should know for whom we are praying, why we are praying, and what we're praying for. If we don't know, and must invent a reason, then we should not continue. We need to trust the Holy Spirit to teach us how to approach each situation. We should always allow plenty of time for guidance and preparation for our effort. Too often we plunge headlong into prayer projects, spraying the air with pious sounding petitions and missing the point of the whole matter. If several thousand prayer groups were to pray in an inner-directed manner, by the guidance of the Holy Spirit, the results would be far-reaching.

I can envision a National Congress of Prayer that would convene at least once a year in Washington, D.C., for the express purpose of concentrating spiritual energies on world problems. This assemblage would include representatives of prayer groups, spiritual life organizations from all denominations. The Congress of Prayer would not assemble to hear lengthy reports, eloquent speeches, or be immersed in time-wasting discussion; rather, it would be a gathering of prayers to pray believingly for specific target goals. We need not wait for a National Congress of Prayer to be inaugurated in Washington, D.C.; Christians in cities, towns, and hamlets across our country should establish local Congresses of Prayer at once.

The people who would be asked to address the National Congress of Prayer would be experienced in dealing with some phase of a particular world problem. Representatives of the State Department, using maps and giving important objective information, would be of invaluable assistance. They would offer the Congress of Prayer pertinent facts concerning our prayer projects. Then the

Congress of Prayer would be led in prayer by spiritual life leaders who would serve as agents for the Spirit of God in launching the delegates on the wings of prayer. Prayer Congresses would be dedicated to the purpose of prayer in its various forms and all other activities would be of secondary importance.

People returning home from the annual meeting of the Congress of Prayer would doubtless be inspired to establish Congresses of Prayer in their own communities. Then, when we were faced with a national or world crisis, local Congresses of Prayer would be called into session. People who believed in inner-directed prayer and other forms of praying would gather together and pray for specific situations. The constituency of all Congresses, national or local, should be interdenominational. The Spirit is no respecter of denominational lines. Prayer is a gift of God. It belongs to all his people. Congresses of Prayer all over America, meeting to direct their prayers on given occasion to specific areas of need, would by the power of the Spirit change the course of history. And if a National Congress of Prayer should prove an effective instrument, why not an International Congress of Prayer?

Frankly, I don't know anything more exciting than the power of prayer. Sometimes when we go into prayer, we carry a heavy burden for ourselves or for other people who are going through a crisis, and our praying can become a pretty serious and somber affair. I once heard a chaplain of a city hospital intoning a vesper prayer. It went something like this: "Oh, Lord, we in this hospital who are plunged into the darkness of ill health—we who feel so weak and alone—we who are broken and in pain...." I tuned him out and went my way wondering what this man's concept of prayer really was.

When you are in a crisis situation, and you're trying to pray, you might return to the story of Peter and John in the New Testament and see how they responded in one of the darkest moments in the life of the Christian Church, when they were given the word by the authorities in Jerusalem to cease and desist from any more teaching, healing, and preaching in the name of Christ. They were also threatened that further violations would be met with severe punishment. I can imagine how devastated they must have felt. Their work, which was to communicate the most important message in all the world, was now under condemnation. After their release, they went trudging off to Mary's house. They knew the disciples and others would be gathered in the upper room to hear what had happened. Once there, they probably unloaded all their complaints about the cruel fates opposing them at every turn. "It's hopeless," they may have lamented. "How can we spread the word if we're constantly being blocked by people like Herod, Pilate, and the Sanhedrin? What's the use of going on?"

The cold chill of pessimism hung in the air like death itself. The stress point had been reached and passed. Once radiant faces were now gloomy and downcast. All at once another voice was heard in that room. An old brother had dropped to his knees to pray and his words were like a burst of sunlight, like the fire of a new creation and finally all the other friends joined with him in his prayer, "Lord, thou art God, which hast made heaven, and earth, and the sea, and all that in them is . . ." (Acts 4:24, KJV).

This is the prayer of triumphant realization. It is a strategy of God that would have us behold the unutterable greatness of God who was here before the earth and the heavens and all were formed and will be here after it has all disappeared. Prayer is the living connection with what is and will always be.

Notes

1. Frank C. Laubach, *Letters by a Modern Mystic* (Westwood, N.J.: Fleming H. Revell, 1937), p. 50.
2. Ibid., p. 52.
3. Jack H. Holland, *Your Freedom to Be* (Salinas, Cal.: Hudson-Cohan, 1977), p. 9.
4. Thomas Kelly, *A Testament of Devotion* (New York: Harper & Row, 1941), p. 29.

CHAPTER 6

The Pathway of Hope

THERE IS no crisis quite like death; and the pain associated with the loss of a loved one is further intensified when we are without the presence of Christ, for it is out of him that flows the marvelous pathway of hope. It is because of this hope that John Donne could proclaim, "I run to death."[1] Or Shakespeare soliloquize, "Ah, tis a consummation devoutly to be wished."[2] Or Sir Walter Raleigh expound, "O eloquent, just and mighty death![3] Or Plato comment, "No one knows that death is the greatest of all human blessings."[4] Or Walt Whitman rejoice, "Nothing can happen more beautiful than death."[5] Or Marcus Aurelius advise, "Think not disdainfully of death, but look on it with favor, for nature wills it like all else."[6] Or a certain preacher who began an Easter sermon, "I wish I were dead." I cannot imagine people expressing themselves so positively toward the ultimacy of death if they had not discovered the hope that springs from Christ.

While hope is implicit in Hebraic-Christian teaching, not all the religions of the world consider it a virtue. Those that metaphysically deny life take a very dim view of hope. For them, it is an illusory path that leads people astray. Neither the Greeks nor Romans listed hope among their virtues. However, from the standpoint of biblical religion, hope is endorsed in both the Old and New Testaments. The Hebrew prophets had unshakable hope for the future. They believed in the coming of a great day when "the earth shall be full of the knowledge of the Lord as the waters cover the sea" (Isa. 11:9). Hope in the Old Testament is based largely on God's mighty work in the past and present which forms the basis for hope in the future.

In the New Testament, Paul's concept of hope enables us to meet any crisis through the indwelling presence of Christ, whom he believed to be "the hope of glory" (Col. 1:27). For the early Christian church, hope was centered in the life, death, and resurrection of Jesus. His living presence at work in the lives of his followers was the ground of their hope, inspiring them to become the pioneers and perfectors of our faith.

Hope is the one outlet for those whose lives have been leveled in times of crisis. By way of illustration, George Buttrick used to tell his audiences that even the most hopelessly dead, closed-in body of water in the world is not without an outlet. The Dead Sea that appears to be a stagnant lake at the foot of the Jordan River Valley is not without a point of departure. There is a way out, and it is up. He explained that potash, that for years has been building up at the water's edge as a waste deposit, has been found to be an incredibly potent fertilizer. It is estimated that if the potash from the Dead Sea could be mined, it would bring life to dead soil all over the world.

This is more than a metaphor in that the hope that we share in Christ is part of the ultimate strategy of God that despite that whatever might appear, there is always a way out—even up.

During World War II, Dr. Martin Niemöller, a Lutheran pastor, ironically came to prominence as Adolf Hitler's personal prisoner. Listening to him tell his story, it is very difficult to believe that such a quiet, peaceful man could have so uncompromisingly held his ground against one of the most evil men who ever lived. Niemöller did not know from day to day whether it might be his last. When Hitler, gesturing wildly and all but frothing at the mouth, made outrageous demands and threatened evil against the church in Germany, Niemöller with calm resolve would respond, "Because there is God, Mein Fuehrer, we can wait. But we cannot give to man the things which are God's."[7] Hitler's personal prisoner, when faced with crisis, was filled with the strategy of hope in Christ that is expressed in 1 Peter 3:15-16: "Always be prepared to make a defense to anyone who calls you to account for the hope that is in you, and yet do it with gentleness and reverence; and keep your conscience clear, so that, when you are abused, those who revile your good behavior in Christ may be put to shame."

The promissory aspect of the hope that bolsters Christians through the crisis of a death comes from some words Jesus spoke to his friends in an upper room. Jesus made certain promises to them immediately preceding his crucifixion. He divulged that in the life to come "in my Father's House," as he spoke of it, "there are many mansions," which suggests that eternal life includes many levels of experience. This is not a mere going on. Many mansions comes from the Latin term *mansoni*, which refers to stopping-off places and suggests the possibility of many planes of existence along the way where truths are taught and experienced in an evolutionary process of development. We will then be involved on the spiritual level with which we have spiritual affinity. I believe that in the next life we are in a progressive learning experience. We are in a growing process. I can think of nothing more uninspiring than mere survival—that is, going on in the same way as before. This is not life, certainly not the life of hope. The life of hope is full of new experience, freed from physical restraints and impediments, opening to new opportunities of spiritual growth.

When Jesus hung on the cross, we are told that a repentant thief on his right (one of the two crucified with him) asked that he might share the life that Jesus would be entering after his death. Jesus' answer is amazing, considering the circumstances. Certainly, anyone could excuse him if for a moment he had lost hope. After all, his physical life was draining out. He was suffering a high fever from the inflammation of his wounds. Congested blood throughout his body had swollen every vein. His body was pain-wracked from hanging in an awkward position on the cross. Three or four nails driven into his body had torn gaping holes in his flesh. In the human sense, we can certainly understand his cry out of the desolation of injury and loneliness, "Father, why have you forsaken me?"

It was during those crisis moments in dying that one of those being crucified with him pleaded for a special blessing. Jesus answered in the most astounding way. Everyone who fears death or who is at this moment facing a crisis hour with death, should read Jesus' words again and again, for in so doing you will be in touch with the overcoming hope that is centered in God. If you believe in him at all, you must not miss what he said from his most excruciatingly painful yet strategically profound pulpit. Not "maybe," not "perhaps," but "*today* thou shalt be with me in paradise" (Luke 23:43).

Paradise here probably refers to a Persian word for royal garden. In fact, something like the Garden of Eden might be a fair comparison. It is not the highest heaven, it is probably more like the third heaven of which Paul spoke. But it means that as of today, that is where they would be. No waiting around for the end of an age. "Today," said Jesus, to of all people a repentant thief, "Thou shall be with me in the royal garden."

In the fourteenth chapter of St. John, Jesus speaks about going to prepare a place for those who are his followers, and that he would return to receive them to himself. The picture this brings to mind is that of a husband and father going off to another city to establish himself in business, and purchasing a house there and making preparation for his wife and family to join him. No doubt Jesus' comment about returning refers to what is known in Christian terminology as the "second coming of Christ." It is the belief of many that history must have an end, and many Christians identify that end with the return of Jesus.

Several times in my life I have heard very specific predictions as to when Jesus would return based on prophetic scripture. To my knowledge, none of these prophesies have come true, but this is not to say that the people making such pronouncements are not motivated by sincerity. However, if you are concerned about such matters, I would recommend that you read what Jesus had to say in this connection: "But of that day or that hour no one knows, not even the angels in heaven, nor the Son, but only the Father. Take heed, watch; for you do not know when the time will come" (Mark 13:32–33).

Several years ago, Professor C. H. Dodd suggested that the second coming is not an external event at all. Rather, it is an extremely personal one. He believed that it marked the beginning of a new history for the person receiving Christ and the end of the age of his old life. The coming of Christ is a coming into a personal experience and it happens when Christ meets us within. Dr. Dodd's approach has a lot of appeal for me; but whether Christ comes in a personal way or at some cataclysmic moment in history, my hope in him remains the same.

I feel a little bit like Ralph Waldo Emerson on this subject, who was often exposed, particularly in religious circles, to doomsday prophecies. One day a man trembling with excitement came at him shouting, "Mr. Emerson! the world is coming to an end next Friday night!" "Oh well," said Emerson quite lightly, "let it come. I think we can get along without it."

Let's get back to how the hope we share in Jesus helps us to meet the critical challenge of death. Often when I am confronted with griefstricken people, they seem to be further burdened by a feeling that because of their grief reaction, they are letting Christ down. I've heard it a thousand times, "If I were a better Christian, I would be stronger." At this point, I want to outline some common grief reactions affecting most of us in this sort of crisis.

As you read these words, you may yourself be in the clutches of a death situation. You may be grasping for some straw of hope as you tumble through a valley of despair. Everything now is as unreal as the chill wind of death blowing hollow through your emptied life. It's hard to get your mind on anything but your personal loss. Part of you has been ripped away. The early days of grief are dark and dreary. You carry a heart so heavy that it is all you can do to even move. Even worse, it is impossible to find words to describe what you are going through because there are no adequate words.

Let me explain a little about natural grief patterns that occur to everyone. This may reassure you that what you are experiencing is completely normal and not indicative of a lost faith. Your hope in Christ will blossom again; in fact, whether you realize it or not, this hope is sustaining you to some extent even now. What I'm recording may not fit your situation precisely, but it will touch the main trauma plateaus along the way.

First there comes a sense of the unreal. You simply cannot believe that your loved one is dead. In fact, a "denial mechanism" comes into play, which is nature's anesthetic to help you through the initial impact. Everything bears the marks of unreality. Nothing is in focus. It is the dark night of the soul and unfortunately, that is where you are—alone without anyone to really understand your situation. People will try to help but they just can't, at least for the present.

Second comes the release of tears. It is important that the tears flow. Tears are like the loosing of rain from a darkened sky. Never listen to anyone who counsels that you "stop crying, because tears won't bring them back." Jesus wept at the grave of Lazarus. Paul counsels "that we sorrow not as those who have no hope!" But nevertheless, even those with hope can and should weep. The release of human tears allows the outer self to ventilate its pent-up shock and anxiety over the destruction of a treasured relationship in your life. This adjustment is best accomplished with the aid of tears.

Recently, I went to be with some friends in our church who had just lost a loved one. The deceased was a very dear and close friend. I knelt to pray with the rest of the members of the family, a prayer of hope that we would soon pass through the dark valley. Despite all effort to contain myself, in the midst of the prayer I began to cry. Those around reached out to comfort me and we all held each other like animals huddled in a storm before continuing with the prayer of hope. What I'm saying is that it is natural, therapeutically helpful, and even necessary to weep when in grief.

The third stage is a period of negative fixation. It is perfectly normal to want to talk and think of nothing but the one who has died. It is never wise to divert this expression, that is, not to speak of your loved one. The bereaved need to talk about their loss. There is an old Jewish custom that the first meal after a funeral is called a meal of consolation. A neighbor should prepare the food. The rabbi should be present and the subject of conversation should be the one who is deceased.

Fourth comes the physical response to grief. All our physical responses are interwoven with the emotions. A gloomy mood can successfully block the work of the physical organism. Emotional upset is a foe to the heart, the digestion, the circulation, every nerve and brain cell. Our body faithfully reproduces an inner hurt. Again, this negative emotion is understandable, but eventually one should realize the harm that is being done to the body by excess grief.

Fifth comes the inevitable period of depression. Someone has wisely commented, "Where there is no faith in the future, there is no power in the present." A depressed state is perfectly acceptable as long as it does not play a permanent role in the adjustment pattern. Once, when Martin Luther was in a state of depression that had lasted several days, his wife came to breakfast dressed in black. She closed the windows, locked the doors, tiptoed in silence. Finally Luther cried out in bewilderment, "Who is dead?" to which she replied, "God is dead." The rugged old reformer got the message. But people who have lost someone close to them should be allowed a period to work through their depression.

Sixth comes the guilt feelings. People in grief remember all the slights, failures, mistakes, real or imagined, in their relationship with the one who has died. They plague themselves wondering if they should have done this or that, or maybe if they had provided more support the person might still be alive. They question if they should or should not have allowed the deceased to undergo radiation treatments or should they have taken him or her to a doctor sooner. They remember the times when they were inconvenienced by the needs of the dying patient, and did not measure up as heroically as they thought they should. At the moment, it is difficult to dispassionately realize that when people are very ill, they can make unreasonable demands on those around them, which later engender guilt feelings in those who could not comply with every wish.

Seventh comes resentment. Doctors, nurses, hospital facilities, family, friends, minister, anyone who was involved in the last days of the deceased's life can be a target of resentment. The bill of complaint is that everyone should have been more helpful, more attentive, more dedicated. Doctors should have been more skillful, should have visited more often, and performed their services more compassionately. The medicines the nurses dispensed were all wrong. The dietician's food was horrible. The minister didn't come to visit enough. Friends of the family were not sufficiently solicitous. Even God, most of all God, seems to have been out to lunch when he was needed most. This is normal rage and will eventually pass.

Eighth comes withdrawal. People develop what is known

as "the cemetery syndrome." Life is still tied up with the body of the loved one, so if the body is out at the cemetery, that's where they go to experience what little there is left in their lives. But, in strictest terms, a cemetery, insofar as the Christian hope is concerned, is not a cemetery at all. In the Christian church of the first century, the place where Christians were buried was called a graveyard. It wasn't until the second century that those burial places were called cemeteries, and that expression has been with us ever since. Graveyards and cemeteries are two different things. The word "cemetery" comes from a Greek term meaning "sleeping chamber," which is not what the Christian hope is about. People are not out in the cemeteries sleeping. Jesus' words to the repentent thief should have ended that notion. He said, "Today thou shalt be with me in paradise." The place where the body or the ashes have been placed is a graveyard. It is not a sleeping place.

There are other extravagances of sentiment and negative emotion to which the grief-stricken subject themselves. It is said that Madame Curie kept the clothing her husband had worn on the day he was killed in the streets of Paris. From time to time she would get out the bloodstained garments and kiss them passionately until one day her sister grabbed the clothes away from her and burned them in the fireplace. Suffice to say the withdrawn person does not want to hear laughter or normal conversation or anything that indicates that life is going on. But again, this is a very human predisposition and it, too, shall pass.

Finally, as the grief is spent, we begin to make our adjustments. There is a story about a friend of psychologist Victor Frankl, who came to the doctor following his wife's death. The man said, "What am I going to do with my grief?" Frankl responded, "What if you were the one in the grave and she had to carry on?" The friend answered, "She couldn't bear it, it would be too much for her." Frankl answered, "Then, you bear her burden. The gift of your suffering is a gift to her."

As the presence of Christ begins to resurface with accompanying feelings of hope, we can begin anticipating the day when we shall be reunited with our loved ones in the Father's House. Gradually, we realize that the separation we are experiencing is not for eternity but only a period of time. Therefore, we may be able to say to that precious spirit who has passed beyond our physical sight, "I'm going to let you go, I'm going to release you. I wish you a wonderful experience in the life ahead. I'm looking forward to the day when I can join you. What a reunion it will be. Wait for me. I love you."

In this process of readjustment, Dr. Albert Schweitzer used to suggest that when he got to brooding or was inclined to pessimism and hopelessness, he always got his hands on a task to lessen the evil in God's world. Some of the greatest strides in personal rehabilitation from grief come in doing something for someone else. When people begin to grapple with redemptive tasks, they feel a part of the future rather than the past—subsequently, their hope returns more swiftly, and this is the strategy of God.

One of the classic examples of a wholesome response to death and dying is found in the Old Testament story of King David. When his child was ill he wept and pleaded with God to spare his son. He fasted and lay on the ground day after day. Finally, the baby died. The King's servants were understandably reticent about informing him. But David, noting their whispering, eventually asked:

"Is the child dead?" and they said, "He is dead." Then David arose from the earth, and washed and anointed himself, and changed his clothes; and he came into the house of the Lord, and worshiped; he then came to his own house; and when he asked, they set food before him and he ate. Then his servants said to him, "What is this thing that you have done? You fasted and wept for the child while it was alive; but when the child died, you arose and ate food." He said, "While the child was still alive, I fasted and wept; for I said, 'Who knows whether the Lord will be gracious to me, that the child may live.' But now he is dead; why should I fast? Can I bring him back again? I shall go to him, but he will not return to me." (2 Sam. 12:19-23)

"We are saved," Paul said, "by hope" (Rom. 8:24). And it is our business as Christians to share our hope in Christ with others. We all need to be more aware of our potential ministry to others who are involved in the agonizing suffering from the loss of a loved one. Travel through your community, and behind nearly every door of every house you will find some pain that death has inflicted.

While in seminary, I was serving a church on weekends. In one of my pastoral care classes, a professor who offered all sorts of valuable instruction was trying to teach us how to help people through the grief processes. He suggested using certain therapeutic words, scripture quotations, and how to conduct ourselves in the presence of people who are caught in the throes of a death crisis. Then came an emergency call from my parish. Someone had committed suicide in the little church that I was serving. I rushed to the disaster scene, equipped with all the good words and pertinent scriptures and pastorly demeanor. Though the family listened to what I was saying, it was obvious that I wasn't getting through. It wasn't because I lacked motivation, it was just that I hadn't learned how to share in the suffering of others. Within a few moments, I was introduced to the big leagues of the Christian ministry.

A white-haired woman who was a member of our church taught me more about how to care for a family in grief than three years of pastoral care classes even hinted. Entering the room where the family gathered, she didn't say a word, not even the religious words I had been taught. She just held people in her arms one-by-one, lovingly and tenderly. She wept with them, let them talk if they wanted to. I can't remember any scripture verses that she quoted. The important thing was that she was totally there just for them. Her love filled the room like a fragrance. There was a Christ-like presence about her. She was the resurrection spirit. She was the personification of Christian hope. I can't imagine anyone being a more effective minister to those people.

Recently, I was presiding at a graveside service. The family had gathered around a coffin situated on a hoist soon to be lowered into a vault. Suddenly it occurred to me that this must be the five hundredth time I've gone through the process of burying still another friend, saying the same things, praying the same prayers, reading the same scripture, in a sense, looking at the same faces, feeling the same deep pain of saying goodbye to a dear one. Then, by a sheer force of will, I stopped the merry-go-round of customary response. It was difficult, terribly difficult, but I took an inventory of what was really happening. I concluded that I was surrounded by illusion. I indicted my physical senses as blatant deceivers. My eyes told me that on the day of the funeral the sun had come up in dawning splendor and would set in a glow that evening . . . none of which is true according to science. My eyes told me that the earth on which we were grieving was flat except for the mountains I could see off in the distance ... again, according to the best scientific information, such just isn't so. My senses told me that the formidable box bearing the remains of my beloved friend was a solid object. I could touch it and see it in a material bulk form—but once more I was being lied to ... according to the laws of physical science, we know that so-called solid physical shapes are really rapidly moving collections of molecular activity. My eyes further told me that the vaulted sky above the cemetery was blue and that the flowers in such profusion around the grave were in a variety of colors all of which is not so—except as a trick of the optical nerve.

Finally, nothing seemed so final and real as that motionless body in the copper-colored casket, but then something in me rebelled. I felt that I had been lied to long enough—and the last thing I intended was to perpetuate a lie. I deliberately began opening to the powerful vibrations of my friend's life as I had known it (in fact, she had not gone so far into the next dimension that those vibrations had vanished). The words that I had finished reading in the gospel, "I will not leave you comfortless. I will come to you," which she had believed so implicitly, brought Jesus so near that I could all but see his face—particularly his eyes. I saw in his eyes the love and vision that sweeps across all time and space. It was as though he was trying to tell me, with a gracious glance, that my friend was not dead ... that her spirit soared beyond my physical sight—that she was moving on in her evolutionary journey through the various levels of consciousness in the next life. From that moment I have not grieved her passing—the crisis is past and the hope in Christ has sufficed.

I have played my part in the game of make-believe

when the angel of death hovers near, refusing to talk of death, even to acknowledge its imminent presence. At one time or another, most people become pretenders against the grim fact of death. Our pretenses suggest that death is too morbid a subject for healthy-minded people to discuss, and we must evade in every conceivable way the harsh implication of its meaning. So when loved ones become desperately ill, we contrive to deceive them as to the gravity of their illness. However, all the masquerading in the world will not hold back the bad news when family and friends, doctors and nurses whisper their poisonous pessimisms within the conscious or subconscious hearing of the patient. More times than I would care to recollect, I have stood in hospital rooms with dying people who are watching a soap opera on television to avoid the unpleasantness of thinking about the real crisis of death.

When people die, they are entrusted into the care of a friendly mortician who will exercise considerable dramatic skill in staging a funeral performance—complete with make-up, costuming, music, scenery, and dialogue for all who attend. There used to be (and still is in some sections of the country) a "lay-out night," during which people gather near a coffin and behold the embalmer's decorative work. Now and then you hear someone exclaiming, "My, doesn't he look natural." "Doesn't she look wonderful—almost better than she did when she was alive. She's better off now. It's really a blessing. She looks like she's just sleeping."

The next day the preacher will arrive and deliver the funeral sermon, which often sounds faintly apologetic. Many ministers reason that it is their responsibility to defend the ways of the Lord, and death puts the burden of proof squarely on them. Remembering seminary training, the pastor may very well guard against mentioning the words "death, die, and dead."

I must confess that I have not always felt that assured when reading the following ritual, particularly in the case of those who have strategically neglected the presence of God most of their lives.

> Blessed are the dead who die in the Lord from henceforth: Yea, saith the Spirit, that they may rest from their labors; and their works do follow them.
>
> Almighty God, with whom do live the spirits of those who depart hence in the Lord, and with whom the souls of the faithful after death are in strength and gladness: We give thee hearty thanks for the good examples of all those thy servants who, having finished their course in faith, do now rest from their labor.

There are times when I would just as soon have dispensed with the ritual and spoken as did the clergyman in the following tale. When old Sam the town drunk died, a few generous citizens of the community decided to give the old fellow a decent funeral. They bought a casket for him, purchased a cemetery lot, and hired a minister for the funeral. On the day of the ceremony, the minister stood before the small gathering and said, "There isn't much I can say about Sam that you don't know already. He was a drunk most of his life and never amounted to much. But as you pass by the casket, I want you to notice how good he looks since he stopped drinking."

I am not always convinced that the deceased is, as it says in the ritual, "in strength and gladness." When reading the ritual for those who have not shared the Christian hope, I feel a terrible wistfulness. What a tragedy to enter the next life so far removed from the faith that could have brought them a sense of eternal life while they were yet in the flesh. However, I cannot impose my mental or spiritual limitations on Almighty God. His heart is infinitely larger than any of us can imagine. His judgment is based on more than we could ever perceive.

If someone were to calculate the cost of the carloads of flowers that are delivered to the average funeral, the amount would be staggering. I'm quite aware that memorials are now being given in place of flowers. This may not be a boon to the florist industry, but it certainly is beneficial to a more spiritual tone in funeral services. I have not been able to accustom myself to the waste of cut flowers that will end up rotting on a grave. I passionately begrudge the money so misused.

The scene of the contemporary funeral has, in most instances, been moved from a church to the more convenient funeral home. This I will never be able to accept. I have been advised repeatedly that the most "practical" place for the service is in one of the funeral home chapels, where family and friends will not be distracted—by what I don't know! Nevertheless, that's what they say. When did the symbols of the Christian faith come to be classified as a distraction? When someone is a member of a church and has attended church regularly, the church is the logical place from which they should be buried.

In the last few years, there has been a great deal of discussion on whether the body of a Christian should be disposed of through cremation. Frankly, I do not feel that this is an important consideration. The resurrection body, after death, is not returned to a physical state. As we have noted in this study, there is a natural body and a spiritual body. It is the spiritual body that enters life eternal, not the physical body. However, there are many people whose feeling for the physical envelope of their beloved is so great that they could not allow it to be incinerated in a crematorium. After having had a behind-the-scenes look at the cremation process, it leaves me a bit squeamish too. One mortician recently bragged about the effectiveness of his cremation furnace. He proudly claimed, "I can burn almost all the bones in one firing." I asked him about the bones that he couldn't burn. He replied, "I have the best grinding machine in this part of the country for those extra tough bones." If you can handle all this, then cremation may be right for you.

The only other reservation I can think of with regard to cremation is the legendary early Christian idea that a person should not be buried for three days. They believed that it took that long for the soul body to completely separate itself from the flesh, which is probably based on the scriptural report concerning the three-day period of Jesus' entombment.

After the funeral service, the brightly polished hearse waits in a nearby driveway for the pallbearers to deposit the casket on the cushion platform through the side-saddle door. At last the casket is secured in the hearse, surrounded by baskets of flowers. I recall an expensive spray of roses with "Dear Old Dad" spelled out in gold letters on a wide crimson ribbon, which added a sentimental touch. Then there was another tribute tied to a flower spray that I've never forgotten, "Good luck Mother."

Under a canopied area, the grave has been freshly dug in the dark earth with the leftover dirt well-hidden beneath a covering of artificial grass. The minister will then read the words of "the committal" while memorial garden chimes play such traditional background music as, "In the Sweet By and By." At length, grave diggers hiding behind thick trees will reappear, lower the casket into the vault, remove the artificial grass, and cover the vault with the good brown earth.

A person was ill, finally died, and has been buried: but was he or she adequately supported by the hope that is in Christ Jesus? Unfortunately, too often the reality of death and subsequently the resurrection hope is evaded by substituting euphemisms for fact. Death, the most unpopular word in the world is given another expression more pleasing to the ear. We say that a person has "gone to his final rest," "passed away," "slipped beyond," "taken his final sleep," "gone West," "headed for the last round-up," "kicked the bucket," "cashed in his chips," "gone to his reward," or as Shakespeare said more elegantly, "shuffled off this mortal coil." But what of the crisis of death and the Christian strategy of hope?

The matter, very simply put, is that if there is no death, there can be no life. All of life is filled with the punctuation marks of death—commas, hyphens, semicolons, question marks, exclamation marks, and a sprinkling of periods—indicating that there are interruptions, but more to come even after the punctuations. If we are afraid of death, we are also afraid of life. In each moment of life we experience creative urges to die to something that is lesser, so that something higher or better may be born. There is purposefulness about creative dying. In the economy of God's plan for us, we die from an old level to be born into an advanced development. An infant dies to be a toddler, a toddler dies to be a young child, a young child dies to be a teenager. A teenager dies to be a young adult, a young adult dies to be an older adult. And the older adult dies, provided the process has not been interrupted, to move into the life beyond flesh. This is the Christian hope.

Death is the instrument of our becoming. The price of becoming is death. If death is seen through the eyes of hope in Christ, it will be received with the welcome of

St. Francis: "Be thou praised, my Lord, for our sister bodily death." If death can be seen as a process that keeps life moving to something greater than before, then its sting diminishes. No sane person would choose to have development forever arrested at the level of a baby, a child, a teenager, a young adult, or even an older adult. Life cries out for higher evolution into the perfection that God has ordained. However we may attempt to stem the tide of aging by efforts to preserve the appearance of youth through the use of hair dyes, plastic surgery, wrinkle creams, chin straps, magic oils, pencil and paint, steam baths, gymnasiums, or sun baths, the fact remains that wrinkles, gray hair, and the settling condition of age should faithfully convince us that we are going ahead to something from which we will not return.

But the question still remains, "What sort of life can we hope for beyond the last door we call death?" Our only real authority on this subject is Jesus Christ, who is strangely silent on how to picture the next life. Only now and then did he lift the veil between this life and the next, and then only for a brief moment. Besides his words to a dying thief and the promise he made to his disciples in the upper room, there is another glimpse of the next life that is discovered by reading between the lines of an experience Jesus shared with his friends Mary, Martha, and Lazarus (John 11:1–44). My assumption is that there was probably no home on earth that Jesus enjoyed more than theirs. We are told that once, when Jesus was at a far distant place, Lazarus became ill and died. After he had received the news, Jesus made his way back to Bethany and was told that Lazarus had been entombed for four days. Tearfully, Mary and Martha informed him that if he had been there, Lazarus would not have died. It seemed there was nothing he could do except to go out to the graveyard for the sake of his friends. As he approached the tomb, he saw the gathering of Jewish women, weeping and wailing, keeping vigil at the tomb, which was their custom. Standing at the edge of the crowd, Jesus began to weep. Great tears began rolling down his face. There was a murmur in the crowd. Someone noted aloud, "See how much he loved him." Another may have commented, "Look, he is weeping for the loss of his friend Lazarus."

Nothing could have been farther from the truth. Jesus wept that day at Bethany not because of the death of his friend but because of the obligation he felt on behalf of his unknowing friends. It was on their account that he knelt before a tomb filled with the stench of death and called a man back from a place where there is no more pain, nor loneliness, nor anxiety, nor distress, nor frustration, nor sickness, nor despair—a place where there was no more death. Jesus wept because he was forced to call a man back from the third level of perfection and fulfillment.

The location of heaven is still a baffling question. We are too sophisticated to believe that heaven is up in the sky. We may declare with some degree of enthusiasm that heaven is within, but we're still not quite sure of what that means. One of the few things I remember from my high school science courses is the fascinating fact of molecular action. All things we see appearing in solid form are, in reality, combinations of molecules moving so fast that it is impossible to see them except in a conglomerate state. Any object that appears to have mass is in reality a collectivity of molecular movement. If, for some improbable reason, molecular activity should cease, then every material substance would vanish.

One day, while casually observing the action of a circulating air fan, I noted the illusion of a solid mass given off by the swiftly moving fan blades. When I disconnected the fan from the electric current, the blades ceased to move and the appearance of activity was no more. In an identical manner, the physical world is largely illusory, while the spiritual world is more likely the true reality. At the moment of our physical death, we may begin to see the actuality of the wider life that has been surrounding us all along that was hidden by the limitations of our physical sight. Heaven is not another place, but rather another state of consciousness. We are "surrounded by a great host of witnesses" (Heb. 12:1), which indicates that heaven encompasses our mortal existence and is no farther away from us than our next breath.

My mother once heard an old preacher say, "Perhaps it is better that Jesus did not tell us much about heaven, for if he had we might not want to go on living here." I firmly believe that, if we could see into the next dimension, we would be so eager to move on that we would want to leave this world without even saying goodbye—as it was with the great clergyman Dr. Sam Shoemaker who, when heading for the hospital and leaving behind his beloved home for the last time, did not look back, not even once. Perhaps when we have reached a higher level of spiritual development we can use Paul's words and truly mean them: "For me to live is Christ and to die is gain " (Phil. 1:21).

The late Glenn Clark, formerly a professor at Macalester College, once told of mailing a questionnaire to several of his students who, after graduation from Macalester, had made significant contributions in their chosen work. One of the questions he asked of each person was: "Has there been a death in your immediate family?" Ninety-nine percent responded in the affirmative. An empty chair in the immediate family circle meant something to Glenn Clark. He claimed that the loved one who had gone ahead into the next life was able, by the power of the Holy Spirit, to release spiritual energy on those left behind. By this they were sustained through the crisis of grief and separation and their creative energies were somehow quickened to move ahead with the work of their lives.

My first reaction to this story was that of disbelief. But experience has since taught me some lessons. Several Christian friends who have lost their loved ones have been remarkably reinforced through their crisis of loss. Many of them, particularly women who have had families to raise, debts to pay, and who were without adequate education and training to qualify for the sort of employment that would help them meet their financial needs, have been for the most part almost miraculously assisted. In each case they received incredible sustaining power. For instance, one woman who lost her thirty-six-year-old husband was faced with the awesome responsibility of raising three young children alone. She is now doing what she would not or could not have done while her husband was alive. She is studying in a teacher's college, making excellent grades, and is on the way to getting her teaching degree. Another woman with three children lost her husband, who was in the real estate business. After much soul searching, she decided to take over his business and has prospered marvelously. She is now doing what previously she had never dreamed she could do. Still another woman, faced with the responsibility of raising her family alone following the death of her husband, has done well for herself in a successful babysitting enterprise that previously would never have been an option. The stories go on and on.

In each case, like Dr. Clark, I have asked a searching question of those people left behind. How did you manage the crisis challenges following your loved one's death? The answers have been amazingly uniform. As one person put it, "It seems my husband was right here in spirit helping me. Doors have opened and the right people have crossed my path with help that has come at opportune moments. I have the feeling that God has taken over my whole life." Again, the power of hope through Christ is demonstrated.

The great Christian hope is that God does not leave us comfortless. He comes to us in a variety of strategically supportive ways. Is it really so surprising that those that have loved us in this life would not continue to love us when they cross over to the other side? A large dimension of our Christian hope is in this interaction. There is concourse between this life and the next. There are so many questions that remain unanswered about life and death, yet we possess a certain instinct for immortality. This fires our hope in Christ.

I want to close this book with a memorable episode. I performed a wedding ceremony for two high school teachers who had joined our church and attended on occasion. They were very much involved in the social whirl of our community, and seemed to enjoy it immensely. Then she became ill and I was asked to visit her in the hospital. He was apologetic about asking for my help. "You know, we haven't been to church in quite a while and we feel embarrassed in having to call on you, but we have a crisis here and we really need your help." He choked on his trembling words. "The doctor has told me that my wife's illness is terminal, and we really don't know what to do."

I suggested we pray about it. He asked, "How do you

pray?" So I began explaining the ABC's of prayer. I told him to address God honestly and openly and to remember that God is our Father—that he is near us—even within us. I told them about commencing a spiritual journey, awakening their inner persons and entering an evolutionary path of growth in Christ. They listened intently. After we finished praying, they thanked me profusely and asked me to return the next day—which, of course, I did. I met with their physician that evening and he gave me the grim diagnosis. He said, "We doctors have done all that we can do. Now it's up to you."

For several days we met and prayed together in the hospital room. The husband would be on one side of the bed, the wife in the middle, and I on the other side. As time went on, we witnessed some hopeful signs. In fact, she appeared to be improving. We rejoiced as the remissions came off and on over the next several months that brought her home from the hospital, sometimes for weeks at a time. But finally her disease flared with such intensity that her physical reserves were no match, and she died.

It was a somber November afternoon that we went out to a grave dug in the side of a hill. Friends and relatives gathered below. The young man and I climbed up to the graveside. The clouds were heavy and gray. A chill wind blew fiercely. For a long time, he stood looking into the grave, not acknowledging my presence. Eventually he murmured, "Come up a little closer." I walked up beside him. Then he turned. I remember his brown eyes clear and intense, surprisingly free of tears. He spoke so directly that I was startled. "She is not dead."

With that, we started moving away from the grave, our arms around each other, heads bent against the whipping wind. Then, almost by a reflex, we pulled apart, leaving just enough room for another person to walk between us. We made our way down that hill and when we got to his car, he opened it and spoke with a voice as old as time itself, "We'll see you later. I promise, we'll see you later." I have not seen him since in the flesh, but my hope, so strong in Christ, is that I will see them both later on.

I knew the crisis had passed. The negative force of death sucking the air of joy and hope from our lives would gradually abate. It would be some time before we recovered entirely from the pain of separation, but hope would return, and with hope joy and with joy life—which I believe is God's ultimate plan.

Notes

1. John Donne, *Holy Sonnets*, book I, section 3.
2. William Shakespeare, *Hamlet*, act 3, sc. 1, line 62.
3. Sir Walter Raleigh, *The Works of Sir Walter Raleigh* (New York: Burt Franklin, 1829), vol. 7, p. 900.
4. Plato, *Apologia of Socrates*, section 29.
5. Walt Whitman, "Starting from Paumanok," *Leaves of Grass* (New York: New York University Press, 1965), p. 23.
6. Marcus Aurelius, *Meditations*, book 9, section 3.
7. From a sermon by J. Wallace Hamilton: "The Motive Power of Hope," Pasadena Community Church, St. Petersburg, Florida, October 12, 1958.

Index

Adam, 21, 22, 57
Aging, 122
Airplane crisis, 29-32
Alcoholics Anonymous, 50
Aligning with God, 76-78, 82, 86, 88, 89-90, 97
Atonement doctrine, 22
Augustine, Saint, 21-22, 23, 24, 25

Barclay, Robert, 32
Bodies, dimensional, 87-88
Breathing exercises, 92
Browning, Robert, 44-45
Buttrick, George, 20, 104

Calvin, John, 22
Catastrophic events, 9-10
Cemetery syndrome, 112
Centurion, Roman, 11
Christos, 52
Clark, Glenn, 124-125, 126
Collier, Robert, 91
Coming to self, 24
Congresses of Prayer, 99-100
Coptic gnostic works, 54
Crazy Horse, 31-32
Cremation, 119-120
Cro-Magnon race, 45-46
Curie, Marie, 112

David (King), 33-34, 113-114
Dead Sea, 104

Death, 103, 105-107, 108-128
Denial, of death, 109
Depravity doctrine, 21-25
Depression, in grief, 110-111
De Testimonio Aninae (Tertullian), 34
Dialogues (Plato), 22
Directed prayer, 96-99
Divided mind, 49-50
Dodd, C. H., 108
Dog attack, 1-2, 5
Donne, John, 103

Eden, 86, 107
Egyptians, 22
Einstein, Albert, 23
Eiseley, Loren, 73
Emerson, Ralph Waldo, 108
Empiricists, faith, 6-7, 12
Epileptic boy, 4-5, 67

Faith, 1-17, 67
Faustian motif, 20
Flowers, at funerals, 119
Food, 79, 81-82, 89-90
Forgiveness, 79
Francis, Saint, 122
Frankl, Victor, 112-113
Funerals, 117-119

Galilee Sea feeding, 89-90
Gilmore, David, 7-8

INDEX

Gilmore, Natalie, 8, 71
Gnostics, 21–22
Graveyards, 112, 120
Great Dane attack, 1–2, 5
Greeks, 20, 22, 104
Grief, 108–116
Guilt, in grief, 111
Gunkel, Herman, 77

Healing, 4–6
Heavens, 78, 87–88, 107, 123–124
Hebrews, 20, 104
History of European Morals (Lecky), 47
Hitler, Adolf, 105
Holmes, Oliver Wendell, 32
Holy Family Hospital, 1
Hope, 103–128
Howe, Julia Ward, 13–16, 36–37

Jacob's well, 69
James, William, 2–3
John, 16–17, 37, 101
John the Baptist, 63

Kelly, Thomas, 91
Kern, Jerome, 26
Kerr, Walter, 26
Kingdom of God, 36–54, 62; and faith, 11–12; and love's lessons, 62, 63, 64–65, 70; prayer and, 79–80, 81; soul and, 32, 34
Klages, Ludwig, 28–29
Knox, John, 22

Laubach, Frank, 82–85
Lazarus, 90, 109, 122–123
Learning, 56–74
Lecky, William, 47
Legalism, 36–41
Lessons, 56–74
Listening in, 91–95
Literacy lessons, 85
Lord's Prayer, 78–80, 82
Love, Christ's, 56–74
Luther, Martin, 22, 110–111

Macalester College, 124
Manicheans, 21–22

Mansoni, 105–106
Marcus Aurelius, 103
Martha, 122
Mary, 122
Mary of Magdalene, 43
Messiah, 52
Metanoia, 48
Mind, 27–29, 49–50
Mindanao, 83
Moros, 83–85
"Moving up" crisis, 70–72

Nag-Hammadi jar, 54
Names, 78–79
National Congress of Prayer, 99–100
Negative fixation, on grief, 110
Newton, Isaac, 22–23
Nicodemus, 37–42, 47
Niemöller, Martin, 105
Noah, 75–76

Palal, 91
Paradise, 107
Pasternak, Boris, 33
Patmos, 16
Paul, Saint, xii; and heaven, 87, 107; and hope, 104, 109, 114, 124; and Kingdom of God, 50–52, 53, 54; and love's lessons, 58–59, 61; and soul, 22, 33, 34
Penfield, Wilder, 26–27
Perry, Edmund, 40
Persians, 22
Persistence, 86
Peter, 58, 70, 101
Pharisees, 40
Phelps, William Lyons, 45
Physical response, to grief, 110
Picturing, 88–90
Pilate, 58
Pilgrims, 78
"Pippa Passes" (Browning), 44–45
Plato, 20, 22, 103
Pollard, William G., 90–91
Potash, 104
Prayer, ix–x, 75–102, 126–127
Prayer groups, 98–100
Prodigal son parable, 23–25

INDEX

Psalm 23, 78, 80–82
Psalm 139, 31
Psyche, 27–29

Raleigh, Walter, 103
Reformation theology, 22
Repentance, 48
Resentment, in grief, 111
Retirement homes, 97
Revelation, Book of, 16
Righteousness, 81
Romans, 11, 36, 104
Runners' clinic, 77

Sabatier, Auguste, 61–62
Sailboat, 71
Salesman's secret of success, 10
Samaritan woman, 69
Schweitzer, Albert, 113
Screen of the mind, 92–94
Second coming of Christ, 107–108
Shakespeare, William, 26, 103
Sheehan, George, 2, 3
Shepherds, 80
Shoemaker, Sam, 124
Signal Hill, 83–85
Simon Peter, 58, 70, 101
Sleeping, directed prayer during, 96
Solomon, 33–34
Soul, 18–34
Speaking voice, 91–95

Staff, 81
Star thrower, 73
State Department, 99
Strauss, E. B., 28
Suffering, x, xi. *See also* Grief

Tears, of grief, 109–110
Teenagers, 97–98
Teilhard de Chardin, Pierre, 74
Telepathic communication, 95–96
Tertullian, 34
Thief on the cross, 106–107, 112
Thomas, Lewis, 27
Transformations, 42–44, 60, 68, 79
Treasure maps, 89
Twain, Mark, 3

Union Theological Seminary, Manila, 82–83
Unreality, of death, 109

Varieties of Religious Experience (James), 2–3
Visualizing, 88–90

Whitman, Walt, 103
Withdrawals, in grief, 111–112
Women, 68–69
Wordsworth, William, 11
World problems, 97–100

Zacchaeus, 65–66